H. Shmuel Erlich, Mira Erlich-Ginor, Hermann Beland
Fed with Tears – Poisoned with Milk

The series »Bibliothek der Psychoanalyse« (Library of Psychoanalysis) wishes to create a forum of discussion which stimulates the basic, human and cultural aspects of psychoanalysis as a science and as a clinical theory and practice. The different currents within psychoanalysis will be given space, and the critical dialogue with the neighbouring academic fields will be intensified. So far, the following thematic focuses have developed:

The rediscovery of psychoanalytic classics which have long been out of print – such as the works of Otto Fenichel, Karl Abraham, W.R.D. Fairbairn, Otto Rank and others – will strengthen the common roots of the psychoanalytic movement, which is threatening to split. Another component of the psychoanalytic identity is the treatment of both the person and the works of Sigmund Freud, and of the discussions and conflicts of the psychoanalytic movement's early days.

In the course of the process during which psychoanalysis established itself as a medical-psychological therapy, it neglected its multidisciplinarity regarding the humanities, cultural analysis and politics. By resuming the dialogue with the neighbouring academic fields, the culture-critical and socio-critical heritage of psychoanalysis will be revitalised and advanced.

Psychoanalysis now competes with neighbouring psychotherapeutic methods and with biological psychiatry more than it used to. Being the most sophisticated among the psychotherapeutic methods, psychoanalysis should face an empirical-scientific verficiation of its procedures and its therapeutical success, but it should also develop its own criteria and concepts to control results. This context also includes the revival of the discussion about the particular scientific-theoretical status of psychoanalysis.

One hundred years after its creation by Sigmund Freud, psychoanalysis faces new challenges which it can only meet by focussing on its critical potential.

BIBLIOTHEK DER PSYCHOANALYSE
EDITED BY HANS-JÜRGEN WIRTH

H. Shmuel Erlich, Mira Erlich-Ginor,
Hermann Beland

Fed with Tears –
Poisoned with Milk

The »Nazareth« Group-Relations-Conferences
Germans and Israelis – The Past in the Present

With a Preface by Archbishop Desmond M. Tutu
Dedicated to Rafael Moses († 2002) and Eric Miller († 2002)

Psychosozial-Verlag

This book is sponsored by the German Psychoanalytic Association (DPV) and the German Psychoanalytic Society (DPG).

Bibliographic information of Die Deutsche Bibliothek (The German Library) Die Deutsche Bibliothek lists this publication in the Deutsche Nationalbibliografie (German National Bibliography). Detailed bibliographical data can be accessed via internet (http://dnb.ddb.de).

Original edition
© 2009 Psychosozial-Verlag
Walltorstr. 10, D-35390 Gießen.
Phone: +49-641/969978-18; Telefax: +49-641/969978-19
e-mail: info@psychosozial-verlag.de
www.psychosozial-verlag.de
All rights reserved. No portion of this publication may be reproduced in any manner without the written permission of the publisher.
Cover: »Die Treppe der Kontinuität im Jüdischen Museum Berlin«
© Jewish Museum Berlin, photo: Sönke Tollkühn
Draft design cover: Hanspeter Ludwig, Wetzlar
www.imaginary-world.net
Printed in Germany
ISBN 978-3-89806-751-5

This book is dedicated to Eric J. Miller and Rafael Moses – colleagues, friends and mentors whose lively presence and wisdom permeate its every page.

Contents

Foreword		11
	Desmond M. Tutu, Archbishop Emeritus, Anglican Church of Southern Africa	
I	Introduction	15
	H. Shmuel Erlich	
II	The Story and History of the Project	17
II.1	Israel Psychoanalytic Society and the Sigmund Freud Center	17
II.2	The Stages of the German Psychoanalysts on Their Way to the First Nazareth Conference	20
II.3	Events and Experiences Leading to the Idea of a German-Israeli Conference	29
III	Structure and Design	35
III.1	The Process of Conference Design	35
III.2	Supplementary Comments on Design and Structure	43

| IV | The Conference Experience
Mira Erlich-Ginor | 49 |

IV.1	Introduction: The Book and the Collage – A Concept and its Problems	49
IV.2	Participants – Present and Missing	55
IV.3	The Conferences Experience	69
IV.4	Looking at the Invisible: The Unthought Known and the Unspeakable	89
IV.5	The Danger/Fear of False Reconciliation	141
IV.6	By way of Outcome – Getting out from the Imprisonment of the Past	147
IV.7	To be staff in these Conferences	158
IV.8	No Way and no Reason to Sum Up	164
IV.9	List of Contributors	166

| V | Central and Emergent Themes
H. Shmuel Erlich | 167 |

V.1	Holocaust-Related Identity Components of Germans and Israelis	167
V.2	Special Trauma and Special Relationships	174
V.3	Change and Transformation – the Burden of Betrayal	177

| VI | Post Conference Experience
H. Shmuel Erlich | 183 |

| VI.1 | Presentations, Discussions, Their Impact and Contributions | 183 |

VII	Epilogue	187
	H. Shmuel Erlich	
VII.1	Where to Now?	187
VII.2	Who Needs These Conferences?	188

References 191

Foreword

*Desmond M. Tutu, Archbishop Emeritus,
Anglican Church of Southern Africa*

When our politicians negotiated a peaceful transition from the horrors of the apartheid era to the genuinely free South Africa that so many of us had, over the long years, argued, prayed, struggled, fought, and laid down our lives for, the joy in our hearts knew no bounds. At last our beautiful land – a land so richly endowed by God with wonderful natural resources, wide expanses, rolling mountains, singing birds, bright shining stars, and blue skies filled with radiant, golden sunshine – would be there for all God's people to share and enjoy. For us this had been so precious a dream that we hardly dared hope it would come true, and yet here, in our own lifetimes, that moment finally arrived. Years of pain, hardship and suffering were giving way to joy, freedom and justice. Nelson Mandela, so long a living symbol of the chains imprisoning our country, was free at last and, as he had vowed, his freedom and that of our country went hand in hand. The magnitude of joy in our hearts that we should be alive at such a moment could only be a gift from God.

Our happiness, however, was tempered by one small but nagging worry: what if the atrocities of the apartheid era continued to live on subconsciously in people's minds? What if these were to fester and breed, and lead in time to demands for revenge and retribution, unleashing once again the dark and destructive forces associated with the apartheid era, turned now on the former apartheid masters, their offspring or their perceived collaborators or beneficiaries? When we looked to precedents in the wider world around us we realised that we had to take seriously the danger of such a grave and worrying outcome, even though it seemed so out of keeping with the generosity of spirit that characterised our new dawn, and try to do something about this.

The Truth and Reconciliation Commission, which I had the honour of chairing, was set up to address this concern. It was based on the hope that if the truth were faced openly, squarely and honestly, this might have the power to heal the wounds of the past and thus to help to bring closure to past atrocities. In the sessions of the Commission we witnessed again and again what a powerful instrument facing the truth is. It brought to life most powerfully the pain and anguish of the victims of atrocities carried out by the apartheid regime (and also sometimes by members of the liberation movement) and by being there we, the commissioners and committee members, could experience something of the cruel and unbearable burden our fellow citizens had been carrying. And we were encouraged by the fact that in many cases, even when the atrocities concerned were so horrific that a wish for revenge might be entirely understandable, the experience of having their stories heard and fully acknowledged seemed to open up a process by which anger and hatred could be mitigated and stilled, helping many victims to find closure, which often involved forgiving the perpetrators and moving on. On the side of the perpetrators, too, one could sometimes see that facing the truth of what they had done brought forth the terrible pain of guilt and remorse. I felt privileged and humbled to be in the presence of such profoundly moving and transformative emotional experiences.

This book reports on the beginning stages of a project that I believe has much in common with the work of the Truth and Reconciliation Commission. It began when a group of German and Israeli psychoanalysts and psychotherapists recognised that lurking beneath a polite and courteous exterior was a deep sense of unease and suspicion in the way they related to each other. This was based not on their own qualities as individuals, but was a general stereotype connected to the Holocaust: Jews could, quite simply, not be expected to trust Germans, etc. It is ironic that psychoanalysts – even German ones – should be stereotyped in this way, since Hitler had branded theirs as a "Jewish science" which he set out to exterminate, burning psychoanalytic texts and driving Freud and most of his contemporaries from continental Europe. If German psychoanalysts of the past could not be uniformly stereotyped as Nazi-collaborators or sympathisers, the accusation against the present generation was even more irrational. It was a true legacy of the past. In the course of their training, psychoanalysts and psychotherapists are required to scrutinise unconscious forces within in order to be less subject to the influence of the irrational, so the existence of these stereotypes in this group suggested that they were very stubbornly entrenched in the mind.

The book describes the systematic attempt of this courageous group to address this legacy of the Holocaust. They refined a psychoanalytic method that relies not on rational argument and debate, but on trying to engage the irrational feelings that underpin prejudice. To do so they create a special "conference" setting, away from the pressures of everyday life, in which each group can face its own most deeply held prejudices, assumptions and beliefs *in the presence of the other group*. In the TRC I was always deeply impressed with how, when victims and perpetrators came face to face, the reality of past atrocities stored in the mind were powerfully brought to life in front of us so that we shared in feelings that were often quite overwhelming. The written record, no matter how faithful and accurate, cannot possibly convey the full, three dimensional texture of these events as they unfold, and I believe that it is one's willingness to be fully involved that carries the potential for healing. Who can fail to appreciate, for example, the sheer depth of feeling and thoughtfulness that lies behind the simple words from a German woman, "I have an ordinary Nazi mother" – reported, incidentally, by an admiring Israeli colleague? How poignant to be able to acknowledge that the tender loving care – the very care that allowed a child to grow into a beautiful human being – coexisted with something more sinister that involved the extermination of others. What unspeakable pain, shame and humiliation must have been faced in recognising the truth that this was indeed part of her inner legacy? I find it tremendously reassuring that she must have felt safe enough in the conference setting for this important work to take place, for, in the words of another participant, "tears are better than blood and words are better than tears".

Being present in these meetings must have been deeply moving, and from my experience in the TRC I can quite see how such involvement may be life-changing, as many of the participants indicate. The process of confronting the truth of how the atrocities of the past live on in the mind helps to bring closure, laying the atrocity to rest. To help even a single individual to achieve this and to normalise their relationship with members of a group that previously oppressed them is an important achievement. Left unattended, it is these very ghosts of the past that can be exploited by unscrupulous politicians for their own cynical gain, as we saw in the 1990's following the breakup of Yugoslavia, and also in the Rwandan genocide. There are quite simply too many wars that build on grievances and prejudices passed down through the generations, and every known method by which they might be effectively laid to rest deserves to be made widely known. This is one reason to welcome the publication of this important book, which I hope will be widely read.

There is a further reason that I am especially pleased to be associated with this work. Since the three conferences reported on in the book there have been significant developments that I very much welcome. First, the membership was expanded from Germans and Israelis to include other groupings affected by the Holocaust, and in the most recent conference (September 2008) work was also begun on the relationship between Israelis and Palestinians. This not only brings in work on atrocities still current in the Palestinian-Israeli conflict, but also opens up the possibility of finding genuine meeting points in a world where enmity between groups is so often the norm. I am thinking, for example, of how polarised not only the relationship between Arabs and Israelis has become, but also those between Jews, Christians and Muslims in general, and what powder kegs they are in our world today. Would it not be wonderful if we found that facing the truth of what lies within can help to normalise these troubled relationships, helping to create a world in which our differences are celebrated rather than being a cause of conflict?

The second development is related to this, in that the group working on these conferences has now set up a new organisation, Partners in Confronting Collective Atrocities (PCCA), whose specific aim is to apply what has been learnt from work that focused on the Holocaust to other atrocities that live on in people's minds. I particularly welcome the fact that what has been learnt from work on the aftermath of the most widely-documented atrocity in human history will be made available for helping others who, though their suffering may be less well known, are equally deserving of our help.

October 2008
Cape Town, South Africa

I   Introduction
H. Shmuel Erlich

This volume aims to make a unique and significant contribution to the proliferating literature on German-Israeli relatedness in the post-Holocaust era. It is both a record and a testimony to a novel and vitally important approach to this work, demonstrating the possibility of dealing with Germans and Israelis in a way that is immediate, direct, and powerfully evocative. The power of this work lies in that it does *not* aim at rapprochement or exoneration. It focuses on the two groups by using highly skilled and trained professionals – psychoanalysts and psychotherapists – from both countries. And it employs a unique methodology – the magnifying lens of Group Relations working conferences. In this sense it may well be said that this volume lies at the intersection of a number of crucial human, social and heuristic developments that have characterized the twentieth century.

This book shows *the unique meaning and importance of the other* to one's own efforts to change. The bottom line of these conferences is a demonstration of how crucial the *actual presence of the other* is in producing the desirable changes in one's identity. This is all the more powerful when this other is not a "neutral" presence but the one to whom one's own identity relates. This cannot be emphasized too strongly. It is one of the major and most poignant contributions and outcomes of the conferences and of this book.

It is commonplace knowledge that Germans and Jews have been marked, perhaps for eternity, by the horrors of the Holocaust. It may also be asserted that this relatedness reaches far beyond that of victims and perpetrators, as it is commonly and somewhat banally referred to. A deep "special" relatedness exists between these two national groups, with deep historical past roots, a most troubled and difficult present, and an unforeseeable future. There have been and are numerous efforts aimed at affecting some sort of understanding and reconciliation between Germans and Israelis and/or Jews. None, however, have used this approach or format, and these particular representatives.

In many ways, this is an impossible task in more than one sense. It is an impossibility to deal with the horrors of the Holocaust, directly or indirectly. There is a strong tendency within segments of German society to avoid the subject of the Holocaust. Within Israeli society, the Holocaust has been socially institutionalized and ritualized, and relationships with Germany and Germans are ambivalently regarded, and even out-rightly shunned. At another level, it has been extremely difficult to describe the moving personal and group experiences of members in Group Relations conferences, the burgeoning literature in this area notwithstanding. Finally, psychoanalysts and psychotherapists are highly individualistic and personal, and typically somewhat suspicious of and alien to working in groups.

In spite of these considerable difficulties, the meeting and work of German and Israeli-Jewish analysts and therapists took place three times between 1994 and 2000. Participation and involvement in these working conferences has grown and become more established in both countries and has had certain small but unmistakable influences on their culture. Above all, however, is the fact that those who have participated in these conferences – members and staff – have been ready to describe their experiences, often painfully and searchingly personal, and always nationally and cross-nationally telling.

It is in this specific regard that the significant contribution of this volume lies: directly and obliquely, it focuses on the meaning and underpinnings of personal and national identity and identifications. It lays bare the pain involved in changing one's personal and group identity. It spotlights the depth and power of prejudice and the tremendous difficulty of unlearning it.

Lastly, the work reported provides a valuable blueprint and a possible methodology for this kind of undertaking. It offers a model for working with extreme conflict groups, between whom the concept of conflict takes on life-and-death dimensions. Such conflict groups abound on the national and international scene. In fact, there is not a day that all of us are not made disturbingly aware of such conflicts and their protracted bloody manifestations. While this volume does not suggest magical formulas or miraculous shortcuts, it does describe a possible approach and a method that may well be applicable to many other conflict situations around the world.

II The Story and History of the Project

Every new endeavor tells a story. Behind the project described in this volume there is a history that sheds at least partial light on the way it was conceived and developed. The aim of the present chapter is to tell this story, to introduce some of the leading actors, to provide the scenery, and to usher the reader through the backstage of the evolving drama.

II.1 Israel Psychoanalytic Society and the Sigmund Freud Center

H. Shmuel Erlich

The Israel Psychoanalytic Society is one of the oldest component organizations making up the International Psychoanalytical Association. In 1935 Freud wrote: "In addition to the older local groups (in Vienna, Berlin, Budapest, London, Holland, Switzerland, and Russia), societies have since been formed in Paris and Calcutta, two in Japan, several in the United States, and quite recently one each in Jerusalem and South Africa and two in Scandinavia. Out of their own funds these local societies support (or are in process of forming) training institutes, in which instruction in the practice of psychoanalysis is given according to a uniform plan, and out-patient clinics in which experienced analysts as well as students give free treatment to patients of limited means" (Freud, S. 1935, p. 73). The Palestine [now Israel] Psychoanalytic Society was founded in 1933 by Max Eitingon, one of Freud's closest students, associates and disciples, after he fled from the Nazi regime in Germany to Palestine (then under British Mandate). As described by Freud, the

Society soon established the Israel Psychoanalytic Institute, which is now named after Eitingon. The Institute was modeled after the Berlin Psychoanalytic Institute, founded by Eitingon and Carl Abraham in 1921, which became the model of training for most psychoanalytic training institutes.

From a small and modest start, the Israel Psychoanalytic Society has greatly increased its membership, visibility and influence. It now numbers about 150 members and boasts another 100 candidates undergoing psychoanalytic training in the Max Eitingon Israel Psychoanalytic Institute. Members and candidates represent a variety of professionals in the mental health area, at this point in time predominantly clinical psychology, and to a lesser degree psychiatry and psychiatric social work. All the members and candidates are actively engaged in treatment, in private practice and the public sector. Many teach in various programs and institutions, and several have university positions where they teach and pursue research interests.

The Society has a lively and colorful scientific life, influenced by all the controversies and disagreements prevalent in contemporary psychoanalysis. In terms of schools of thought, it might be noted that while in the beginning and the first few decades the Society was strongly representative of and influenced by Central European, mostly German psychoanalysis, in later years it has been influenced by American Ego Psychology, followed by British Object Relations, and then again by American Self Psychology and more recently by the Relational and Intersubjective approaches. One can find the entire gamut of psychoanalytic thinking playing active roles, ranging from Neo-Freudians, Kleinians and Middle Group to French Psychoanalysis and contemporary Relational perspectives.

The inception of the Sigmund Freud Center at The Hebrew University of Jerusalem is closely linked with the historical roots of the Israel Psychoanalytic Society. After Max Eitingon's arrival in Palestine, Sigmund Freud, who was on the Board of Trustees of the Hebrew University of Jerusalem, wrote to its president, Judah L. Magnes, suggesting the creation of a Chair for a professor of psychoanalysis, and named Eitingon to be its occupant. The proposal was turned down by the Senate on the grounds that psychoanalysis could not be considered a science. Freud was offended and thereafter no longer referred to the Hebrew University as "our university".

In 1977 the International Psychoanalytic Association (IPA) held its biannual congress in Jerusalem, for the first time outside the continental boundaries of Europe. To celebrate the occasion and repair the rupture between Freud and the Hebrew University, the IPA made a gift to the university, endowing the Sigmund Freud Chair in Psychoanalysis. Three years later, more funds were collected and the Sigmund Freud Center for Psychoanalytic Study and Research was created. Several well-known international and Israeli psychoanalysts held the Chair between 1980 and 2005 for varying periods and served as Directors of the Freud Center. Under their leadership the Freud Center organized international conferences on questions that brought together psychoanalytic thinkers around various substantive issues. One of these conferences is of particular relevance here as a forerunner of the conferences that are the subject matter of this book and will be described below.

Group Relations Conferences

The Tavistock Institute of Human Relations of London conducted since 1957 working conferences designed to explore group relations, usually under the overall heading of *"Authority and Leadership"*. These annual conferences were referred to as the "Leicester Conference" after what had been their venue for many years. The conference was an experiential experiment in group relations, employing a unique methodology that combined psychoanalytic ideas about transference, projection and regression together with inputs from open system theory.

What is a Group Relations Conference?

This unique combination resulted in a conference in which members, who sign on voluntarily, take part in several kinds of predesigned events (e.g., Small Study Group, Large Study Group, Plenaries, an Inter-Group and an Organizational or System Event, as well as Review and Application Group). The staff conducts itself in role, interpreting what is going on in the here-and-now events on the basis of their experience, and also acting as the conference management with responsibility for maintaining the boundary conditions and adhering to the primary task. The method provides members with numerous opportunities to learn from and through their own experience about such phenomena as leadership, the exercise and delegation of authority, conscious and unconscious group processes, the place and meaning of boundaries, of task and role, and of fantasy relatedness as against actual relationships with other groups. The learning takes place entirely through one's relevant experiences and there are no didactic aspects.

OFEK – Group Relations Work in Israel

In 1985 a working group was formed in Israel by several people who had become interested in the Group Relations methodology developed by the Tavistock Institute. This group had first or second hand experience with such conferences both at Leicester and in the USA, where this work was introduced in the 1960s. The group soon formed itself into a registered nonprofit organization named The Israel Association for the Study of Group and Organizational Processes (IASGOP). This somewhat unwieldy name was later on changed to OFEK – Organization, Person, Group (the acronym works in Hebrew). Connections were established between OFEK (IASGOP) and the Tavistock Institute Group Relations Program. The latter, under the directorship of Dr. Eric Miller, assisted the Israeli group to mount and conduct its own Group Relations conferences. Beginning in 1987 OFEK has conducted annual international, English speaking Group Relations conferences under the general banner of *Authority and Leadership*. In addition, it offered Hebrew language conferences on *Authority and Leadership*, as well as conferences on specific subjects and social phenomena. OFEK has greatly grown in numbers and its membership currently includes non-Israeli members who live in other countries.

II.2 The Stages of the German Psychoanalysts on Their Way to the First Nazareth Conference

Hermann Beland
Were there any specific inner and outer stages on the German psychoanalysts' way to the Nazareth Conferences? The history of the state of mind of such a small collective as that of the German psychoanalysts must be conceived

as embedded in the history of the German post-war generation's conception of itself regarding the significance of the Nazi period and in particular the remembering of the Holocaust. This had to be the aim of the German psychoanalysts as well. The most important experience of the decade preceding the conference was this: Only in the presence and through the motivated support of an Israeli/Jewish colleague could German analysts gain a deeper emotional awareness of how they are involved in the past insanity of the annihilation of the Jews in Europe and the intended annihilation of the Jews worldwide.

Unfortunately, the defensiveness against such awareness is still collectively effective. There still is a collective lack of convincing insight into the insanity, into why the Germans wanted this, to what degree they have acknowledged it, and whether they do collectively regret it. I am going to describe below how the collective defensiveness of German analysts as a group gradually diminished enough for the members of the German Psychoanalytic Association (DPV) and the German Psychoanalytic Society (DPG) to be able to hope that through participation in these group relations conferences they may get in touch with aspects of their psychological reality shaped by the past.

The historian Jörn Rüsen has differentiated between three consecutive states of mind of German society concerning the realization of the Holocaust. As the first post-war mentality he identified in the second generation a strategy of "concealing knowledge and extra-territorializing", followed by "moral distancing" from the parents' generation. Through dissociation from National Socialism and counter-identification, this generation had developed an illusionary deep sense of unity with the victims. It is not until a third era, the beginning of which Rüsen dates approximately at the time of the German reunification, that he sees symptomatic signs of a "historization and acknowledgement" of the Holocaust as the beginning of a German integration of identity: "We were the perpetrators" (Rüsen 2001).

The First Post-War Decades: The Inability to Mourn

The history of the mind set of the German Psychoanalytic Association (DPV) during the preparation for the first Nazareth Conference will be described here as the history of *collective* emotional experiences. It is necessarily a deeply subjective attempt. The material on which it is based are all the historical publications on German psychoanalysis since the end of the war and my close personal participation in these collective processes since 1960. The small group of analysts concerned demonstrates Jörn Rüsen's trichotomy particularly clearly, which in this case is tantamount to emotional authentication from inside. The DPV, which will be primarily focused on, in the first thirty years after the war was collectively unable *as a group* to feel its own entanglement in the expulsion, dehumanization and killing of the Jewish population, which it might have felt particularly close to in terms of the fate of its own Jewish members. The "inability to mourn", which Alexander and Margarethe Mitscherlich diagnosed in German post-war society, was not yet collectively grasped and acknowledged as a problem by the psychoanalytic group. As a recognized body of analysts, it somehow did not see itself as belonging to the Germans who were unable to mourn. In retrospect, this is hard to understand. However, one has to keep in mind that the unhappy awareness of individuals has always been something quite different than the collective awareness. As regards contents, the individual awareness anticipated the collective one by decades. As group members, however, those distressed Germans also experienced the collective paralysis, which as individuals they could believe they had left behind long ago. Therefore, the preparation for the Nazareth Conferences included as a prerequisite the often made and proved, quite strange experience that the individual process is always also dependent on collectively held unconscious defensive attitudes.

The small collective of the German analysts had been divided into the German Psychoanalytic Association (DPV) and the German Psychoanalytic Society (DPG) since 1949. The history of this split is to be mentioned here only insofar as it is part of the emotional history of the Nazareth Conferences. During the first two decades after the war, it was not clear what influence the Nazi era and an *unconscious* collective feeling of guilt had had on this split. Both groups were in the collective German state of denying an incredible depression, marked by the imputations of having betrayed Freud and having adapted to the Nazi ideology during the twelve years of dictatorship. Both groups retrospectively inferred from their paranoid enmities an unconscious collective-depressive strain that affected them after the war. What was even more important was the not clearly understood significance of the DPV's recognition by international psychoanalysis in Amsterdam in 1951. The DPG's non-recognition seemed like an international condemnation of its members and increased the enmity against the rival. The DPG seemed to have been allotted the depressing burden of the German past for both psychoanalytic groups. New DPV members, on the other hand, could entertain the semi-conscious illusion of being on the side of persecuted psychoanalysis, and therefore almost belonging to the persecuted ones (cf. Rüsen's second phase). This illusion became part of the identity formation process in psychchoanalytic training during the twenty-five years after the DPV's foundation. It collapsed after the International Psychoanalytic Congress in Jerusalem in 1977, when the German representatives extended an invitation to come to Berlin and did not realize until it was rejected that the shadow cast by the "Final Solution" affected not only Berlin but also the German analysts.

Since the International Psychoanalytic Congress in Hamburg in 1985 it has been possible to observe a rapproachment between the two German analytic groups. In view of the German analysts' main task of acknowledging as individuals and as a group their involvement in the murder of European Jews, which they became aware of only in the 1980s, the memories of mutual reproaches and the DPV's international preferential treatment had lost importance. It was possible to conceive the clinical and theoretical differences as being reconciled during an integration undertaken sometime in the future. On their way to the first Nazareth Conference, which eventually took place in 1994, the reconciliation of the two formerly hostile groups of analysts had essentially been achieved. The German conference members came from both associations and learned at the conference that their membership in the DPV or DPG was inconsequential for the encounter with the Israeli/Jewish group. During the decade before the conference, both groups shared the experience that collective defensive attitudes were emotionally removed only by active willingness and in the presence of Israeli/Jewish colleagues who wanted to meet their German colleagues and were prepared to share their own working through of their histories.

The Second Phase: Between Projection and Acknowledgement

In the decade between 1977 and 1987, serious group tensions within the DPV document a changed collective process. Several publications revealed the true nature of the decision to apply the Nuremberg Laws to their Jewish colleagues, which the "Aryan" members of the Berlin Psychoanalytic Institute had made in the 1930s ("Psychoanalysis in Hitler's Germany" by Lohmann and Rosenkötter, 1982; "Psychoanalysis and National Socialism" by Brainin and Kaminer, 1982; "Capitulation Before the *Weltanschauung*" by Dahmer, 1984). In a tormenting way it was possible, gradually and collectively, to become aware and experience how ashamed and depressed we German analysts were. Collectively and step by step, we became aware and began to feel how bound up and inexorable we had to consider ourselves because of the expulsion of our Jewish colleagues and the legacy of the *Reichsinstitut*. There began a passionate controversial examination of the partial intellectual collaboration, the collective holding responsible and feeling responsible, the anti-Semitic family legacies, the shameful Christian past of anti-Semitism, the irretrievable losses, such as the loss of one's values. The collective conscience of the DPV members was torn between the wish for moral dissociation from the accused (psychoanalytic) fathers' generation and the extremely reluctant acknowledgement of shared responsibility.

The crucial help for the acknowledgement of personal responsibility for the German analysts came in 1983 from Hillel Klein and Rafael Moses. It came in a special way, quite different from the decades of support by prominent Jewish colleagues from England, the Netherlands and the USA who had never explicitly connected German analysts with the Nazi era. As Israeli colleagues, they were heard as the representatives of all Jews worldwide. Talking to their German colleagues about the decades of their own psychological work with which they had tried to win back the lost objects and themselves from inner destruction, they opened up ways which the Germans had not thought possible for themselves or which they did not feel entitled to ("From Guilt to Responsibility" by H. Klein, 2004). Both colleagues became unforgettable good objects that could be internalized. Meeting them made the beginning of a different future possible.

Both colleagues were confronted with a German group that had started to acknowledge its responsibility for the Nazi era. This occurred in moving group experiences in Bamberg in 1980, in Wiesbaden and Cologne in 1983, in Wiesbaden ("Psychoanalysis under Hitler – Psychoanalysis Today") in 1984 and in Wiesbaden (discussion about "Guilt Bearable and Unbearable") in 1988. The insights gained were reinforced in partly polarized, partly remarkably reflexive plenary debates in which many hundreds of members were present.

In the emotional experiences during the discussions of bearable and unbearable despair (1988), the collapse of identity illusions (1984) and collective moral strain (1980) a new, still insecure and shaky way of seeing oneself gradually emerged within the plenum of German psychoanalysts. In the DPG a very similar process took place, paralleling the one in the DPV. These were collective emotional experiences that were necessary as an expression of the integration of collectively split-off, extremely stressful memories. Amnesia and denial started to come loose.

Three Examples of Collectively Made Experiences

In retrospect, it is clear to an objective observer that before these group experiences there was an unfathomable and unreal quality of emotional amnesia among individuals and a denial of their own reality in German groups. An older Dutch analyst expressed this at the end of the discussion in Bamberg (1980) approximately like this: He had not been to Germany since the end of World War II, but he did not regret having travelled to the congress despite his scepticism. There was some collective working-through occurring here which impressed him with its honesty and openness and which he had hardly believed the Germans were capable of (N. Rossier, 1982).

In Wiesbaden in 1984, Rolf Vogt succeeded in providing a remarkable summary of the experience shared by almost all the analysts: "When I joined the DPV, the thing that particularly impressed me was something about the atmosphere. There was a constant feeling of a dead and rigid quality that seemed to hang over all utterances like a thin and impenetrable veil. ... When Hillel Klein talked to us in this room one year ago, I could suddenly understand this impression of mine: The veil was torn apart, the dead and rigid elements tipped over into an excitement of tremendous vibrancy, which literally shook the plenary meeting. Something quite essential had been touched upon. The mute, speechless background had started to move and in a flash revealed part of its significance: ... that we are the heirs of Hitler not only in a historical sense but also in a psychological sense, i. e., we actually and deeply are still his heirs in our own lives. *Hitler's heirs are embarking upon the heritage of Freud. The one heritage mixes with the other like fire and water*" (R. Vogt, 1986, p. 435).

I would like to preserve the memory of another experience the DPV's plenary group had during a discussion, which was essential to the perception of a paranoid group consciousness of collective guilt and to a temporary transformation of this paranoid consciousness of guilt into a depressive one. This discussion, too, once again confirmed the law that we German analysts were able to emotionally realize a further aspect of our participation in the Holocaust only in the presence of Jewish colleagues. The discussion spontaneously occurred at the end of the lecture discussions with Ron Britton, John Steiner and Michael Feldman during the DPV conference in Wiesbaden in 1988. The guests complied with the Germans' need for discussion about the subject of the weekend conference on Guilt Bearable and Unbearable in London in 1986. The German analysts had felt that their English colleagues had taken up the crucial German topic with this contribution to the International Psychoanalytic Congress in Hamburg in 1985, and had gratefully appreciated it. The discussion in Wiesbaden revolved around the analytical task of supporting desperate patients with real guilt whose despair is unbearable for the patients themselves without reducing the inner and outer realities. The experiences of the three guests illustrated that only through the empathic presence of the analyst who accepts the intensity of the pain about irreparable damage and inward aggression but does not leave the patient to him/herself might the pain become more bearable. It was an extremely meditative discussion of the group of several hundred members, the plenum being confronted with a description that simultaneously applied to its own situation as a group and to the situation of its individual members. This discussion, too, was a kind of small-scale anticipation, a deposit on a collective reality that might become possible some time in the future.

The discussion in Wiesbaden in 1988 was probably the most important step in the DPV's collective awareness prior to the Nazareth Conferences, where – it was silently hoped – it would be possible to individually realize and acknowledge the collectively loosened potential in individual work, once again helped by the presence of German and Jewish groups. However, two further necessary stages in the history of the preparation of the Nazareth Conferences remain to be described: 1. the Jerusalem Congress of 1988 on "The Meaning of the Holocaust for Those Not Directly Affected" as well as 2. the plan for a self-experimental research group which Rena and Rafael Moses on the Israeli side and Wolfgang Loch and Hermann Beland on the German side tried to realize together (the "Project").

The Last Stages of the Preparation: the "Project" and the Small Groups in Jerusalem in 1988

Soon after the Hamburg Congress, Rafael and Rena Moses suggested to try something in a research group that had neither been realized at the congress nor anywhere else before: to make it possible to experience and explore the unconscious convictions and feelings held by German and Jewish colleagues in their juxtaposed involvement in the Holocaust. In their opinion, at the Hamburg Congress the international psychoanalytic community had fearfully avoided allowing the necessary emotional collective expression that should have been part of the first post-war congress in the country of the Holocaust. The research project was intended as a self-experiment. A few Israeli and German psychoanalysts were to meet in two groups – one Israeli and one German – and stay together for three years. On approximately six weekends a year, the participants were to meet for discussion in a German-Israeli double group, talking as openly as it was possible for analysts. Both groups would mutually pursue contentious ideas and fantasies that refer to the history of both peoples and particularly to the Holocaust, and would mobilize the appropriate collective defences. The discussions were to evolve in alternating phases of emotional experience and common interpretation and subsequently be examined, revealed and reflected upon in a deepening process of discussions and further meta-discussions. All group discussions were to be recorded and transcribed for the following meetings as part of the working basis. It was expected that as a result of the alternating phases of experiencing and understanding, the participants would become aware of, understand, and perhaps be enabled to overcome that which had collectively and unconsciously dominated both peoples, both the persecuting and the persecuted one. It was planned to publish the scientific results of this psychoanalytic group research. Beyond this, a more ambitious expectation was that once it had proved to be a useful self-experimental research method for conflict resolution between Germans and Jews, the same procedure would be applicable to other political and national groups in conflict. The realization of this plan failed, because none of the existing foundations in politics, business, science and society, neither in Germany nor in Israel, were willing to provide the necessary financial resources. In the summer of 1989, we had to accept that our last chance of being supported by the Stifterverband der Deutschen Industrie (Association of Donors and Foundations of German Industry) had disappeared. At that time, another initiative had already taken form. German and Israeli psychoanalysts were to be given the opportunity in modified Tavistock/Leicester Group Conferences to personally make their collective unconscious conflicts experienceable in the presence of the other group. The scientific project continued for a while to run parallel with the preparations for the first Nazareth Conference. In spite of its eventual failure, the project was definitely part of the preparation processes on the German side.

In 1988, Rafael Moses and Yecheskiel Cohen organized the international congress of the Sigmund Freud Center in Jerusalem on "The Meaning of the Holocaust for Those not Directly Affected" in which a small number of German analysts also participated. Gottfried Appy from Stuttgart, Germany, then president of the DPV, held one of the three main lectures. His psychoanalytic attempt at defining the inner-psychological status of the Holocaust as an inner object ("metaphor") provoked a deep controversy which continued during the work of the small groups. In the discussions of the small groups, the German participants for the first time experienced the function of the presence of the other side in both aspects. Some of them made the impressive experience that they served a catalytic function for some of the Israeli/Jewish group members and that in this respect, they, too, were essential to the experiences of the Jewish group members. Therefore, it was consistent that it was decided in the evening of the last day of the congress to dare to organize the Nazareth Conferences. The discussion took place at the home of Mr. and Mrs. Moses. Rena and Rafael Moses, Jona Rosenfeld, but above all Mira and H. Shmuel Erlich, were the active participants in the discussion on the Israeli side who made the Leicester Group Model seem plausible for the conflict between the two peoples to the German participants and convinced them that they first had to gain experience with Leicester Conferences before the first Nazareth Conference could be organized. The above-mentioned experience in the small groups was at the basis of the German analysts' preparation for the Nazareth Conference, even though it was as yet difficult if not impossible to formulate the Germans' "usefulness" to the Israelis/Jews at the planned conference.

The Experiences as Expressed in the Historic Preamble of the Conference

All of the previously discussed stages in the history of the German analysts that preceded the Nazareth Conference eventually contributed to the experiences formulated in the preamble of the brochure of the first conference:

> "This was the background which led to the idea of a conference of German and Israeli psychoanalysts, in which members of each group might use the other in order to get in touch with deeper elements of their own reality; especially with those elements bound by shared emotional defences, which need the other group's presence to be elicited and diminished. It was suggested that the favourable combination of three factors might provide deeper access to the memories and pains of both peoples: a) The beneficial conditions for learning through experience by Tavistock-type Group Relations Conference; b) The wish shared by all members of such a conference to attempt to better tolerate and bear the memories and conflicts of both peoples by experiencing oneself in this conflict; and c) The professional sensibility of psychoanalysts for emotional and unconscious processes, as well as their tested professional conviction that the pains of unbearable guilt and unbearable mourning are unbearable if borne alone."

II.3 Events and Experiences Leading to the Idea of a German-Israeli Conference

H. Shmuel Erlich

In 1987 Rafael Moses organized a conference under the aegis of the Freud Center, titled "The Meaning of the Holocaust for Those Not Directly Affected by It". Several German analysts took part in this conference, as well as a few from other countries. This marked the first time that German analysts were formally invited and actively participated in a conference in Israel. For many if not most of the Israelis who attended, all from the mental health field and many of them first and second generation offspring of Holocaust survivors, it was a novel and startling experience to meet Germans and speak with them on a close and personal basis. It was similarly a moving emotional experience for the Germans, who came to Israel with much fear and trepidation. While the conference stirred up and released many feelings and experiences, it could not really process or work them through because of the way it was designed and organized: There were psychoanalytic lectures in plenary on Holocaust related topics, and small discussion groups into which the emotional upheavals were channeled. But these materials could not be worked with because of the unclear mandate and the lack of a unified, overall primary task. Nevertheless, this conference provided a genuine first attempt on many levels that called for further work.

At about the same time, connections were formed between the Freud Center and the Ulm psychoanalytic research group. This led to a cooperation which developed into mutual visits and an invitation to Shmuel Erlich and Mira Erlich-Ginor to participate in the Ulm psychoanalytic "Ski Seminars". In the three years in which SE and MEG attended this seminar, especially in the informal time, there was considerable pressure for sharing very personal and interpersonal experiences with them. What stood out was the poignant need of German colleagues "to use" the presence of this Israeli-Jewish couple to unburden themselves of feelings they had never been able to discuss with others, and not even in their personal analyses. In fact, there emerged an unspoken collusion of German analysts to leave the years of the war and persecution untouched in training analyses, in clinical case presentations and in family histories.

The lesson from these difficult experiences was that German colleagues badly needed the actual presence of their Jewish/Israeli counterparts to be able to begin to work through their difficult Holocaust-related personal and professional burdens. SE and MEG were certain that a parallel need existed on the Israeli/Jewish side. As both were founding members of OFEK, with considerable experience in Tavistock Group Relations conferences in Israel and abroad, they focused on this methodology as offering the most promising and suitable way for approaching and working on these highly charged issues with both Germans and Israelis.

There were numerous reasons for selecting this route. Group Relations methodology is psychoanalytically informed and makes use of concepts and phenomena such as transference, projection and splitting. It was thought that this would make it amenable to psychoanalysts, who were at first the exclusive target population. Furthermore, the structure of the conference offers clear and strong boundary conditions which would help contain and protect the work with the anticipated enormously destructive fantasies and powerful emotions that might be unleashed. In addition, the stress in the Group Relations approach, unlike most group dynamics events, is not on an "emotional experience" of a cathartic nature, or on achieving intimacy and closeness, but on *learning from one's experience*. Some work with Germans and Israelis had already been done in which the emphasis was on producing "understanding" with subsequent "forgiveness" and "reconciliation". The Group Relations method, in contradistinction, provides a relatively "safe" setting in which anything that members may wish to address may come up, and the attempt is to understand and interpret systemic dimensions and unconscious processes, fantasies and defenses, with the aim of learning about and from these.

Much work was still left to be done once the decision about using the Group Relations method was reached. Unlike their Israeli counterparts, the German analysts who were involved had no previous experience with this method. This presented considerable obstacles to communicating about basic aspects of goals, method and envisioned outcomes. It was deemed mandatory that the German colleagues acquire such experience as soon as possible to enable them to become full partners and for the work to continue. This they did, attending international Group Relations conferences of OFEK and the Tavistock Institute and gaining the experience needed to be on staff.

A still more difficult problem was the adaptation of the Group Relations method itself to the special requirements and constituency of the proposed conference. This task was assigned to Dr. Eric J. Miller of the Tavistock Institute, who had been unanimously chosen to direct the conference. The decision was based on the ongoing experience and joint work with Eric Miller, one of the most experienced people available worldwide for this kind of work, and his active role in the setting up of OFEK and its early conferences. Eric Miller was charged with coming up with a design that would employ Group Relations methodology in a conference that was decidedly different than the usual one in two important respects: rather than being open to all interested people, this conference was aimed and recognized at the outset two distinct conflicted nationality groups – Germans and Israelis. And instead of the usual focus of learning about authority and leadership in groups and organizations, this conference had a very different aim which at least overtly and formally had nothing to do with such issues, and needed to be defined. Eric Miller tackled this task together with colleagues in Jerusalem and Berlin, working within an international network that presaged the working group as well as the working mode that supported the conference. His description of how the special design and structure of this conference evolved will be found in Chapter 5.

Evolution of the Work on this Volume

As with the conference, the inception of the idea of this book and its pragmatic development followed a long and somewhat erratic evolutionary route. The idea of a book on the conference was first suggested by Shmuel Erlich, then Director of the Freud Center, who saw this project as not only a worthwhile contribution to Group Relations work, but as a unique application and model of employing a psychoanalytic approach to deep seated, irreconcilable issues of hatred, prejudice, violence and enmity. Hermann Beland, Rafael Moses and Eric Miller soon expressed their agreement and support for this project.

The next step was to approach the members who had participated in one or more conference, to inform them about the proposed publication and to enlist their support. It seemed clear from the beginning that a volume written solely from the point of view of the organizers and staff of the conference would be didactic, flat and lifeless. The contributions of members about their personal experiences before, during and after the conference are the real substance of this work, its flesh and blood, so to speak. Accordingly, a letter was sent to all past members, asking them to contribute something in writing about their conference experience. Because the idea and plan of the book have not yet been thoroughly worked out, these instructions were not sufficiently clear from the point of view of an eventual editorial policy. The response was nevertheless very impressive: many people responded, in both German and English, writing pieces of varying lengths and focusing on different aspects. The most striking – and also most problematic from the editorial point of view – was the fact that most of the writers felt they needed to describe the special structure of the conference in detail – the various events, the boundary conditions, the tasks involved, and so on. This was quite redundant and not very useful.

The continuation of the work from this point was beset by numerous obstacles, the most difficult and upsetting being the untimely deaths of both Rafael Moses and Eric Miller, to whose memory this book is dedicated. But it was quite literally revived by Mira Erlich-Ginor, who joined the editors shortly before these deaths. Not only did she take it upon herself to provide much needed spirited encouragement and diligent prodding, but she came up with the conception that resolved the difficulty about how to make use of the widely varied and redundant contributions of the members. She also provided a solution to a puzzlement that has been with us since the idea first came up: How to render a view of a conference in which everyone has their own unique experience without being either unnecessarily uniform, over-generalizing, or repetitively boring? She conceived the idea of an experiential "collage" constructed out of excerpts from members' descriptions, and centered around themes, processes and events. With this she succeeded to give life to very personal statements, as well as to illuminate events from different vantage points, rounding out the picture and giving it greater vigor and depth by juxtaposing differing perspectives and subjectivities. The collage provides the centerpiece and beating heart of this volume.

Finally, we had to find a publishing house that would be interested in carrying out this project. Our initial efforts with a New York publisher were close to completion when the horrors of 9/11 shifted their attention to more immediate atrocities and away from our project. Indeed, one of the poignant issues we met in the course of the trials of finding a publisher, but also in a myriad of related ways, had to do with the fundamental question of the pertinence and relevance of the Holocaust to the present, and the tendency to minimize it by advancing a comparative view of the terror, violence and atrocities beset so many parts of the world. This is a serious issue which will be addressed in the closing chapters of this book.

We were therefore very happy and grateful to receive the acknowledgement and acceptance of our work by the Psychosozial-Verlag (Psychosocial Publishing House). Not only did they agree to publish the book in German, but they also committed themselves to see to its simultaneous publication in English. For this we are most grateful. We firmly believe that this volume serves a highly charged and important cause, not only for those directly involved, i.e. Germans and Jews, analysts and mental health professionals, but for the much wider circle of mankind.

III Structure and Design

III.1 The Process of Conference Design

Eric Miller
It was in the spring of 1992 that I had the privilege of being invited to serve as director of the first German-Israeli conference. A small group of psychoanalysts from the two countries had for several years been working towards an encounter of this kind; now I was to be in charge of making it happen: a privilege indeed, but also a daunting challenge.

My qualification for this role was my experience in the field of Group Relations. I had become involved in this work since shortly after The Tavistock Institute mounted the first "Leicester Conference" in 1957 and I had been joint director and later director of the Institute's Group Relations Programme since 1969. From the mid–1980s onwards I had helped with the formation of the Israel Association for the Study of Group and Organisational Processes (IASGOP; later OFEK) which began to sponsor similar conferences in Israel, including an annual series of international events cosponsored by The Tavistock Institute. The Israelis taking a lead in the Israeli-German initiative were founder members of IASGOP.

As many readers will know, the "Leicester model" (Rice 1965; Miller 1989) provides a series of settings for the experiential study of group behaviour in the here and now: Small Study Groups (SSG) of about 10–12 members with a consultant; a Large Study Group (LSG) comprising the total membership – typically between 40 and 75 – with 2–4 consultants; an Intergroup Event (IG) in which participants form into groups and study the conscious and unconscious processes that develop between them; and an Institutional Event

(IE) which explores the relatedness of the two groups – the membership and the staff as management – that constitute the conference as a whole. In addition, there are Review Groups (RG), Application Groups (AG) and Plenaries (P) to enable members to reflect on their experience in their conference roles and to explore its implications for their roles in institutions outside. During the one or two weeks of such a conference there are several sessions of each kind.

In July 1992, Shmuel Erlich and Rafael Moses each prepared quite a full draft of a brochure for the kind of conference they had in mind and sent copies to Hermann Beland and to me for comments. Other colleagues in Israel and Germany were also consulted. What followed was an intensive interchange of faxes between Berlin, Jerusalem and London which continued over several months. Through this we arrived at a shared view of the enterprise on which we were embarking and all of us learned much from the process.

The differences between the Erlich and Moses drafts were minor – for example, whether the length should be four days or five – rather than substantive. One version spoke of members gaining a greater "understanding ... of their feelings and fantasies in relation to the complex factors affecting the relationship between Germans and Jews", while the other was more explicit in describing the relationship as one of conflict. They were however in complete agreement that this should be a Leicester-type conference using the same set of events described above and the same methodology.

On this, I had reservations. The design of the earliest Leicester conferences was strongly influenced by theory and methodology derived from psychoanalysis (e.g. Klein, 1959) and extended by the work of Bion (1948–51, 1952, 1961), who had shown that a quasi-psychoanalytic role – interpreting the transference – in a group setting could reveal significant insights into primitive unconscious group processes. Bion's group-as-a-whole perspective was amplified in the early 1960s by open system theory (Rice, 1958, 1963, 1965; Miller and Rice, 1967), producing a conceptual framework later called "system psychodynamics" – a framework that informed the work of Rice, myself and other colleagues in consultancy to organizations. Rice recognized that the evolving designs and methodology of the Leicester conferences, with the emphasis on interpreting the transference of members onto the consultants, were centrally effective for the study of authority: through examining their feelings and fantasies and their consequent projections onto consultants as authority figures members were gaining insights into their own experience of taking and giving authority in leadership and followership roles. From that time onwards, the title of most Leicester conferences became *"Authority, Leadership and Organization"*, and conferences based on this model have almost always included the word "authority" in the title. Correspondingly, the primary task of the conferences is generally defined in some such terms as this:

> "To provide opportunities to study the exercise of authority in the context of inter-personal, inter-group and institutional relations within the conference as a temporary organization."

My reservation about the Erlich-Moses proposals was that the study of authority was not the central purpose of the German-Israeli conference (though, as they and Beland later pointed out, nor was it irrelevant: for example, in that the constructs of authority and leadership in German culture may have been a factor in the Holocaust). If we could be clearer about the aim and primary task we would be able to draw on the system psychodynamics framework to arrive at a more appropriate design. The framework is plainly used differently in organizational consultancy, and the Group Relations Program had devised other designs for conferences on specific themes, such as men and women at work. This new conference needed to be seen not so much as a "daughter of Leicester" – in my Israeli colleague's language – but as a "cousin of Leicester".

To clarify the primary task I raised various questions. The first, based on the concept of the open system as being engaged in processes of importing, transforming and exporting, was: What is the desired output? To quote from my fax:

> "In what role will members be applying their learning? As individuals? As people with a particular nationality? As psychoanalysts? Or what? Or, to put it another way, are we primarily hoping for personal learning or professional learning? In the present formulation [i.e. the proposals from Erlich and Moses] with its emphasis on Israelis versus Germans, Jews versus non-Jews, my inference is that the underlying primary task is some kind of cathartic experience that will mobilize German guilt and reparation. It is also a false polarization ... [For example there are] German Jews ... and German-born Israelis."

I went on to offer a tentative formulation of the primary task:

"To provide opportunities for participants to explore how feelings and fantasies about 'German-ness' and 'Israeli-ness' influence relations within and between the two groups in the conference."

This, as I saw it,

"would express a broader aim of exploring how these issues relate to individual members' roles both as citizens and as analysts. If that were our aim we would want members to go away with both experiential learning and some conceptualization."

The response from Jerusalem was constructive:

"Our feeling is that we would want to emphasize first and foremost the personal and experiential learning, and only after that the professional side. The German-Jewish polarization exists, but should not lead simplistically to the mobilization of guilt, reparation and catharsis. The experience will hopefully contribute to a more variegated, diversified and personalized experiential learning in all members. Admittedly, that will be difficult, but this is the challenge of this particular conference. They approved the definition of primary task but sensibly proposed adding the third identity of 'Jewishness'."

This was also confirmed by Beland. Now began the debate about design. My basic proposition was that the design needed to recognize both the national difference and also the shared professional identity of the members as psychoanalysts. I had the idea of including some conceptual work as a means of reinforcing that shared identity. It also would counterbalance the strong pull of the perpetrator-victim dynamic, which is something that Beland had reflected on in his response to the original proposals from Jerusalem. I had floated some preliminary ideas about the events of the conference along with my initial formulation of the primary task and in a late-September fax I took them further. First I reiterated that:

"Whereas, when we are studying authority, the transference onto staff directly expresses the issue, in this case we have to be studying how participants use staff as consultants and as management in their struggle to relate to each other over the Jewish issue. Consequently, although some events may have the same names as at Leicester, the context of the task changes their character."

I went on to elaborate my specific proposals:
- Small Study Groups (SSG) would have mixed nationalities. There would be six sessions and each group should have the experience of three sessions with a German consultant and three with an Israeli. (The question of staffing is discussed below.)
- Large Study Group (LSG). Whilst both Erlich and Moses had assumed inclusion of this event (and were to continue to argue for it), I was reluctant: "I cannot see the place of a LSG with this bifurcated membership and this task." That was the rational argument, but I was also anxious. A large group, whether in a conference or in "real life", is notoriously volatile and I saw it as posing serious and risky issues of containment. Instead I opted for an increased number of ...
- Plenaries (P), which would give both members and staff together opportunities to review the current state of the conference institution and their relatedness to it.
- As an alternative to IG/IE I proposed a System Event (SE), explicitly designed to explore relationships and relatedness a) within and between the two national sub memberships and b) between them and staff as management. ("Relatedness" refers to feelings and fantasies about one's own group and the other group whether or not they are interacting with each other.) The SE would open with the two nationalities in separate groups.
- Review Groups (RG) and Application Groups (AG) would have about six members of the same nationality (the same composition for both) and the AG would be focused on members' external roles as psychoanalysts.

I prepared a draft timetable incorporating these proposals. The three-way debate continued. Neither Berlin nor Jerusalem liked the idea of switching consultants in the SGs. To quote Moses:

> "While we can see the usefulness of studying the different transferences to the two different consultants we feel strongly that this would introduce an element of instability and restlessness that we would like to see avoided."

Given my own anxieties about containment, I readily agreed. Separate openings for the SE were approved by Moses but questioned by Beland. His experience in his own psychoanalytic institution in Germany was that in meetings explicitly to explore their German past, "we needed the presence of our Israeli or Jewish colleagues in order to be able to feel parts of our own reality which is related the Holocaust", and he believed that the same applied to Jews. That was an important point. Indeed, it was the recognition that each needed the other that had generated the idea of this conference. But I was not convinced that it was an argument against separate openings for the SE.

My proposals for same-nationality composition for RGs and AGs were also questioned. Moses recommended mixed nationalities for both, and Beland for RGs. My provisional program had proposed that the conference should end with a P followed by an AG. Beland recommended changing this into an RG "which would be designed to understand the last Plenary. I think it possible that the whole conference will come to some sort of solution during this last Plenary, which final result might well need to be reflected on and understood consciously." Here I quote in full my response to these issues:

> "First, I very much appreciate the point about the discovery and rediscovery of the need for the other in order to get in touch with deeper elements of one's own reality – I think we are all agreed that we would like our members to go away at the end of the week with new insights into their own realities that they can take home into professional and personal lives in Germany and Israel. I have tried to design into the conference process a series of iterations of that joining together and going 'home'. That is why I want single-nationality Review and Application Groups. Thus on the morning of the second day, after having been together in the Opening Plenary and then, interactively, in three SSGs, members will be going into a first RG essentially to explore the question: 'What is the state of my German/Israeli identity now?' (My prediction is that in any case there will be a tendency between events for same-nationality dyads and triads to get together informally: I want some of that activity to be recognized as part of the work of the Conference.) I see the System Event as a second beginning. Members have first arrived at the Conference in their separate groups bringing with them quite complex motivations and expectations; and we as staff have put them together in the P and SSGs. Now at the opening of the SE they are starting again in their separate groups, but this time, although some staff will he present as consultants, the members have to use their own authority to decide

whether and how to relate to the other. I see this as a potentially significant learning experience, because it evokes again the question of why they came to the Conference (and by now the answer may already be a little different) and they are put in touch with the mixed and quite probably ambivalent feelings generated over the first 24 hours: wanting to meet the other 'out there' and yet not wanting to meet the other in oneself. From then on, I would expect the encounters to take on a new quality. This, then, is my reason for not wanting to relieve members of the responsibility for exercising their own authority in the SE: they need to give themselves the authority to engage in a new experience and to learn. Besides providing consultants, the task of the staff group as management in the SE will be to interpret the processes in the system as a whole, using the dynamics of the staff group itself as a significant source of data. After the SE, in the last two days we have further iterations of mixed SSG and Plenary sessions separated by same-nationality RG/AGs. Hermann may be right in believing that the whole Conference will come to a sort of solution in the final P. I suspect that this points to an unconscious wish that many members may bring to the Conference, for a 'final solution' – Germans and Israelis each wanting to get rid of the internalized other. I am hoping that this design will produce more of a cumulative, stepwise and continuing process of learning (though there may he backward as well as forward steps!) rather than a final resolution or revelation. The experience needs to live on within the members, not be left behind."

Writing that helped to clarify my own thinking and the thinking of my colleagues too. I quote part of Beland's response:

"Thank you too for your interpretation of my hope for a solution. That wish, to get rid of the internalized other, exists and is deep-rooted. It is the negative core of the whole thing, and it has been so, throughout history. If this interpretation becomes an experienced insight of many members of the group, attained by the work of the conference, I would look on it as one of the hoped for results of the conference. Now you put it at the beginning and I see again that the conference has already begun."

That was a wise comment. In this planning phase, it was as if we were a mini-staff group working with an imagined membership and it was a significant learning process.

One product of the process was an agreed design (Figure, see below). We also had an agreed title: "Germans and Israelis: The Past in the Present. A Working Conference for Psychoanalysts." Interspersed with our debate on design were practical discussions on date, location and also staffing.

Staffing in fact turned out to be an important element in the design. My obvious qualification for directing this conference was, as mentioned earlier, my track record in Group Relations. A second, less explicit, qualification was that I was non-German, non-Jewish and also not a psychoanalyst. In relation to the German-Israeli polarization, I represented a third, an "other". (Beyond that, as a Briton, historically I represented an enemy of both: of Germany in two world wars and of the emergent state of Israel during the British occupation of Palestine.) I saw the role of the "third" as important in holding on to some degree of detachment and providing sufficient containment to enable the members to work at the difficult issues that would arise rather than acting them out, and I did not want to be alone in this role. Accordingly, we recruited Kathleen Pogue White, a black American psychoanalyst from New York, as associate director and another British woman, Evelyn Cleavely. Ideally I had also wanted the presence of both Germans and Israelis in consulting roles, so that the staff group itself would be able to reflect and work at some of the issues that would be preoccupying the members, and fortunately we were able to achieve this. So we finished with a staff of four Israelis (including the administrator, Jona Rosenfeld, who was well experienced in Group Relations work and who also acted as a consultant to a RG/AG), three Germans, and three "neithers". To help them join "the conference that had already started" they all received copies of the interchange of faxes.

A year after the first conference most of the staff were able to meet in London to review the experience. Although questions about the design were raised, it was subsequently agreed to make no changes for Nazareth II either in the design or in the staffing. In the event, recruitment did not justify such a large staff, so each of the Israeli, German and "neither" subgroups was reduced by one.

Evaluation of a conference has to be largely subjective. Did the process of moving from event to event *feel* right? Did it provide members with opportunities to engage with the primary task? Did it enable them to learn? Some of the answers to these questions may appear in other contributions to this volume. One other question is: Did the staff learn? Speaking for myself, I certainly did.

Provisional Program
P = Plenary, OP =Opening P, CP = Closing P
SE = System Event
SSG = Small Study Group
RG = Review Group
AG = Application Group

	DAY 1	DAY 2	DAY 3	DAY 4	DAY 5	DAY 6
9.00-10.30		SSG	SSG	SSG	SSG	CP
10.30	COFFEE					
11.00-12.30		RG	SE	SE	RG	AG
13.00	LUNCH					
14.30-16.00	OP	SE OP 15.00-16.00	-------	SE	AG	
16.00	COFFEE					
16.30-18.00	SSG	SE	SE	SE	SE CP	
18.30-20.00	DINNER					
20.00-21.30	SSG	SE	SE	-------	AG	

Figure: Konferenzdesign

III.2 Supplementary Comments on Design and Structure

H. Shmuel Erlich

The challenge presented by the German-Israeli conference was a doubly difficult one: it called for a conference designed for two distinct nationality groups, rather than the usual open and mixed recruitment. Even more difficult was the fact that it directly addressed the two groups entangled in the most devastating, onerous and asymmetrical conflict of the twentieth century. To put a group suffering from persecution, victimization and annihilation together with the group carrying the burden of responsibility for perpetrating these sufferings was a formidable task, and required everything the Tavistock Group Relations model could offer. There is no doubt that Eric Miller succeeded in pulling this off very impressively. His work on the structure and design of the conference is no less than ingenious. It represents a masterful application of the essential parameters of Group Relations theory, technique and accumulated experience to a novel and most unusual situation.

The best proof of the strength and viability of the design and structure which Eric Miller created is that it actually worked very well and continued to do so for three successive conferences – the first two in Nazareth, Israel and the third in Bad Segeberg, Germany. Nonetheless, there were certain hitches and flaws in the design which in time called for rectification and change.

The most striking and controversial issue was around the Plenaries. One of the significant deviations in Eric Miller's design from the usual or typical Group Relations structure was his decision not to have a Large Study Group in this conference. This was a premeditated choice on his part, motivated by anxiety and apprehension about the potential explosiveness of the encounter between the two nationality groups of Germans and Israelis. Despite all the precautions, such as aiming (and at first limiting) the membership to psychoanalysts, on the assumption that they might be better equipped to contain the difficult emotions that would be set off, the fears and anxieties generated by the prospective encounter were undiminished. This was definitely true of all who were connected with the project before the first conference. But the anxiety and destructive fantasies did not subside even by the third conference. A poignant illustration of these proliferating fantasies ha s to do with this conference, which was held in Germany: The female German conference administrator suggested to her Israeli male co-administrator (German born and German speaking) that she should accompany him to town so as "to protect" him from potential assault and unpleasantness.

The impact of these fears and fantasies on Eric Miller's design was to opt against the inclusion of a Large Group as one of the conference events. Since

Large Group dynamics are extremely volatile and unpredictable, it was felt that this event should be avoided at all cost. Instead, the design made use of five Plenaries spaced over the duration of the conference: an opening and closing plenary, and three additional ones interspersed in between.

In a number of ways the structure of Plenaries is significantly different from that of a Large Study Group: In the latter all members participate, but only a few (usually 3–4) members of staff are present as consultants, and the conference management roles are therefore not represented (members may of course attempt to mobilize staff in their management roles). The seating arrangement reflects this –participants are seated in some kind of circular pattern, and consultants take seats among the members. In the Plenary, on the other hand, all members as well as all staff are present, and the seating is much more structured and formal: the staff is seated as a distinct and well defined group, facing rows of members. Furthermore, the role of staff is not as clearly defined in the Plenary: they tend to speak as individuals, but from their "staff role". This typically results in a more interactive, rather than consultative posture and atmosphere.

Eric Miller's preference was clearly for employing Plenaries instead of a Large Study Group. This decision may well have been wise at the initial stage and may have helped to contain and control the anxiety about the prospective explosion, but it proved to be problematic as the process developed. Members acted and expressed themselves in the Plenaries as if they were actually in a Large Group, but it was considerably more difficult for staff to take up a clear role, and they oscillated between an interactive and a more reflective stance, injecting a note of unclarity into the work. More importantly, the defensive stance underlying this strategic choice did not help to allay the anxiety and confusion, and may perhaps have added to it. Moreover, as with any defensive maneuver, it contributed its share towards augmenting and amplifying the anxieties that were about.

Once again, the proof was in the step eventually taken and its consequences: from the third conference on, a Large Study Group was introduced, which contributed greatly to the work of the conference, without having any ill effects. The five Plenaries were reduced to one Opening and one Closing Plenary. It must be remembered though that a notable developmental shift has taken place from the first conference to the fifth, each conference building and expanding upon its predecessors. It is indeed difficult to compare and judge the anxiety that prevailed before the first conference with the relatively far greater certainty and self-assurance that developed later on.

Another issue connected with the original design was the notion of two clearly defined nationality groupings. This notion was a basic assumption of a kind, and the foundation for much of the pre-conference thinking and planning. Once the conference started, however, it became readily apparent that this was more of a state of mind or fantasy on the part of the planners. Most members easily fitted the two clearly defined categories of Germans or Israelis. But equally obviously, there were individuals who did not neatly fit these definitions and their presence challenged the claim that the world could be divided in this way. For instance, there were Jews who lived in Germany, whose identity was quite complex. There were persons who answered to more than one European citizenship and primary identity. There were some who were the offspring of mixed marriages; and so on. Among the Germans there was no uniformity in a number of ways (including their psychoanalytic identity and allegiance), and the Israelis were also a mixed and varied group. The Primary Task of the Conference specified feelings and fantasies about "German-ness" and "Israeli-ness/Jewish-ness", and of course such fantasies could exist and be pursued without regard to clearly defined identity lines. However, the evidence of the existing complexity within the membership group was a formidable challenge to the underlying binary division the conference design envisioned.

It should be added that the adverse effects of ignoring these complexities was already present at the pre-conference stage. It was openly and angrily stated by a group of German-Jewish analysts living and working in Germany, who felt excluded by the conference stress on "Israeli-ness". This justified complaint led to the publication of an Open Letter in the *Psyche* addressed to the German-Jewish analysts during the pre-conference stage (Erlich, S. 1999).

The need to address and include Diaspora Jews became increasingly prominent with time and led to the first real shift in the conference definition and title. Nevertheless, the conference formal design continued to work with and stress the two main nationality groups, in a sense ignoring the evident complexity. In the conference dynamics, however, there was a shift toward expanding the major reference groups.

A final point on the vicissitudes of the structure and design of the conference has to do with the issue of staffing. It is noteworthy that Eric Miller's initial notion of a staff made up of Israelis, Germans and "Others" (or as he called them "Neithers") proved to be a remarkably robust insight for the structure of the conference. It reflected the bi-national composition the first three conferences directly aimed at. At the same time, it provided an important "third" and otherness to the matrix. This added richness as well as containment was directly connected to the staff group and its internal dynamics, and gradually infiltrated the conference as a whole.

In retrospect, this aspect of the design may perhaps be regarded as more significant than the particular choices and arrangements of groupings and events. The significance of this element cannot be overestimated. It is safe to reflect that it enabled the eventual shift that took place from the fourth conference onward, which openly and expressly addressed the "Others" in the conference title as well as in the dynamics unraveled within the System Event. At a deep unconscious level it may even be seen as incorporating Eric Miller's presence as "The Other" into the conference structure, following his untimely death after directing the third conference.

IV The Conference Experience
Mira Erlich-Ginor

IV.1 Introduction: The Book and the Collage – A Concept and its Problems

The collage – Many Voices, Many Names

The idea to publish a book on the German Israeli Conferences came some time after the first Nazareth Conference back in 1994. It is quite unusual for this kind of Conferences to produce a book, it is almost counter-indicated: the conferences are essentially a "here and now" event, experiences are mainly subjective and the learning remains to the individual's authority. So why is this conference different from all other conferences? We felt that the process as a whole, starting from the initial formative stages, through the different stages of realizing it leading to the experience of the first conference and the following ones carried within them a message that was beyond the individuals that initiated the conferences or took part in them. This message is a lesson to be known and shared by the larger community.

Each conference is a unique and organic entity, having its own past, its present and a future. There is no "official" history of a Conference, no "right" version of what went on. There are conference-narratives as numerous as the number of participants in them. With this in mind we chose to ask participants to write and contribute to a would-be book from their various experiences. Many of them did so. Some contributions were part of presentations participants did to their own professional communities, mainly in Germany. Other contributions were written especially for this book. Sometimes different participants refer to the same event giving complementary, different or even contradictory views of it. In line with the notion of "no true history" I gave as many narratives as were available to the same event. The reader is not invited to make up her mind and choose a preferred version but reflect on the complexity of what an experience is: how meaning is created out of raw material of information, projections, past experiences, present state of mind and so on.

Authorship

Whose book is it anyway? We see it as "our" book, "we" being all the participants of the conferences: members and staff, Germans and Israelis. The book reflects the conferences as a collective enterprise. On the basis of this understanding participants contributed their material and authorized the editors to create the "collage".

It took several years and three more conferences to be ready to publish the book. For a long time it was not clear how to do justice to the wealth of material that we received. There was much redundancy, since each writer felt obliged to provide the whole context and frame. The idea of a "collage" made it possible to use the material in a selective way: additive, even interactive, rather than repetitive, with the aim of giving a lively exposure, as well as the widest possible one.

The work of cutting and pasting contributions is an interpretative act: by choosing, selecting and juxtaposing, new meaning is given to the material. The meaning is personal and subjective: no two people would have done the same "collage". This puts a heavy burden on the interpreter. Cutting out from a written whole does inevitably some injustice to the contributors. My support and at times my consolation was the knowledge that it is a shared enterprise in which I have been authorized by both my co-authors and mainly by the contributors, to do this work on behalf of all of us. It was with a full awareness of the delicacy of the material and the preciousness of the written words that this was done.

The image of a "collage" reflects the working of the conferences which is about creating and deciphering the meaning of what transpires: each person contributes in words, images, acts and feelings from a personal level. Yet these reactions become triggers that produce further reactions that may or may not have meaning to that individual. This is also the way the conference is evolving and developing.

Each contribution holds multifarious meanings, according to the beholder and to the focus at a given moment. My introduction at the beginning of each chapter is in italics.

Every one has a name

It was not clear how the names of the contributors should be mentioned. One possibility was to leave the contributions nameless and to list them in a separate space; another possibility was to have each contribution signed by its author. A heated debate developed in the Internet site of the German-Israeli Conferences (http://atar.mscc.huji.ac.il/~gic/). Below are some excerpts from it:

***

"Hesitating first, I think the idea of a collage is a good idea. We all have our personal impressions, feelings and thoughts about the Conferences. A collage may be the best way to find a broader scope.

The contributions of the participants have to be reduced to personal experiences and the editors have the right of the choice and of shortening. That is o.k. It should be done in contact with the contributors, who should keep the responsibility for their personal impressions.

The problem is the proposed anonymity of the participants who contribute. It means to de-individualize them. It should be a collage of different voices. Let us speak with our own tongues and with our own names.

Four weeks ago I wrote my proposal to the editors. I told them that I can't take part under the condition of anonymity. I hope the question is still open to discussion, and I think the Open Forum (in the German Israeli internet site) is the right place to do it" (Carl Nedelmann).

***

"And – besides being a member of the Conference – the most important thing for me was to write down my experience and to give it to an audience – this was an important process of working through – so may be I can live with some anonymity afterwards as well" (Thea Wittman).

***

"The collage idea is a creative way for a comprehensive and coherent picture – in words. The job that will be done by the editors is enormously complicated, without the 'no-names issue'. I deeply appreciate the effort and I trust that the choices ('selections' …) that will be made are for the benefit of the final product.

In the same time, I can see Carl Nedelmann's association of no-names collage, as de-individualization, as another appearance of 'past in the present'. What I would like to add is my concern about the 'present in the present' argument for no-names.

To say 'we made a decision … to treat the material', has an aroma of patients-therapists, or pupils-teachers patronizing relations. And, I see no need to 'enhance the openness with which (I) will be able to present (my) personal experience' – by no-name writing.

I think that this was not in the conscious minds of the editors, but, this time, let me (participant) give this possibly relevant interpretation for the editors (staff) consideration.

Anyway, if the idea will be to keep the no-name collage, regretfully, I prefer not to participate" (Yoram Hazan).

***

Following this debate we reached the consensus that "every person should have a name" and that each contribution will be signed. It was also important to allow a choice for those contributors who prefer their names not to be mentioned.

The headings try to cover as much as possible the full range of the experiences. The idea of a collage rather than a puzzle implies that there is no correct place for each piece. The decision to what heading to attach each piece was clearer for some contributions, less so for others.

To write or not to write? – That Is the Question

It was not easy for participants to write up their experiences. As mentioned above, these Conferences are experiential: people reach deeply into their inner selves, touching on issues of their personal past, their identities, their personal and collective history, their relations to parents and other meaningful persons, their anxieties, their sources of shame and hope. To share these experiences outside the conference-context in a way that will be communicative to "outsiders" takes courage, determination and the readiness to expose oneself.

Apparently it was more difficult for Israelis than for Germans (there are 16 contributors out of the 65 German participants as compared to 6 contributors out of the 32 Israeli participants). Israeli participants explaining their reluctance to write said repeatedly that "it is too personal". But since the German contributions were also very personal, it seems that the difference lies somewhere else. It may be more difficult for Israelis to write publicly of their experiences because it feels to be a betrayal of themselves and their parents' generation. It was difficult enough to experience it, but to write it up was inconceivable.

As diverse as the contributions are in tone, style and content, they do have something in common: they all came from members that had to some degree a positive experience. Regrettably, we don't have the voices of those who had different, more complex or negative experiences. The invitation to write was sent to all participants, many of whom sent their contributions, and the Collage includes segments of each of them, including some disappointments and criticism. Yet to write a contribution is already to invest in the common project, and it is probable that participants for whom this was not a good experience refrained from contributing to it all together. We can only acknowledge and regret this bias. In addition to the contributions to the Collage the material used contains also letters to the editors and citations from the "GIC" Open Forum on the website.

The contributions speak for themselves and need very little comments and annotations.

***

"It is one day to the deadline. What shall I write, what do I *want* to report? My first idea is that it is impossible to describe my experiences. It is like after psychoanalysis: an intense feeling, the heart full of it, but how to speak about it to someone who did not have this experience? And it takes a lot of courage to think that it will be published" (Eva Mack).

***

"There may be a lot of reasons, why, even after two years, I struggle in vain with contributing something to a publication. One of them is the following: I felt certain uneasiness about the intended publication, which brings into public something which is an inner experience and has its effects internally, like every analytic experience.

The group-experiences were of eminent personal importance and in my former opinion need not and could not be adequately demonstrated to a greater public. Meanwhile I feel less rigid about this point, because the Nazareth-Conference was so important to me, that I tried at least to write about it" (Jutta Matzner-Eicke).

***

"Let's begin at the end. In discussion with friends and letters to and from German colleagues following the Nazareth conference, the expression 'a traumatic experience' comes up again and again. It is thus difficult to get rid of the sense of a leaden weight accompanying the writing of these impressions. It seems to me that I ought to keep them to myself, or share them only with people I am very close to.

Then why am I making this effort to write them down? First, it's a direct continuation of an attempt (which began with the conference) to touch the cold-wall between two territories each of which is filled with great suffering. The strong resistance to touching this wall is understandable. Whenever I touch it, something inside me is undermined. Sometimes, perhaps most of the time, it was my wife and children, or at best my dog, who sensed that I was more than a little bit crazy because once again something had drawn me to get involved with this issue. On the other hand, I found that I gained something essential and very precious whenever a zone that had been hazy became clearer – even if only to a small extend – than it had been before.

Second, this is my little victory over what happened there. Destruction does not win in a place where people fight to find the human in the other, and who can be more 'other' than Germans and Jews? This fight is worthy of having presence in the written word as well. The same words they used as an instrument for distorting reality can now be used to express what really (in my own subjective reality) happened between the Germans and Jews in Nazareth" (Yoram Hazan).

***

"I can say just a very tiny bit of what I feel about the Conference, not because I don't want to tell but because it is very hard to find a way to speak. It is so sever, and so big, so extreme – how can I write about something of this kind?

My problem is how to 'put' in letters and sentences even a bit of what I went through before coming to the conference in Nazareth, during the conference and what is happening to me since. Time passing has its effect as well: a re-closing-up doesn't it?" (Pnina Weisman-Zahor [letter to the editors])

IV.2   Participants – Present and Missing

The title of the Conference refers to "Germans" and "Israelis". This was found to be a stereotypic and somewhat prejudiced point of view. When actually meeting the people who carry these labels, the complexities and intricacies of "Who is Who?" come to the fore: Israelis with roots in Germany, German-Jews, and other partial identities. What follows gives the feeling of who the Israeli are in their own eyes and in the eyes of the Germans, and similarly of who the Germans are; but what about the Jews? The question of "Who is Who?" is a question about identities and parts of identities, sometimes appreciated sometimes hated and depreciated; at times it is felt like a burden that one carries without respite, at other times as a source of pride.

What follows are some profiles of Israelis and Germans who met to work together in the conference. These are people who came together because "our parents would not sit together"; whose parents "met" in a terrible past time. We witnessed many stories in which the actual parents of the participants would not sit together in an actual or symbolic way even today.

It is a challenge for the present generation to "sit together and mourn together".

***

The Baggage and the Burden – Identities and Identifications

"Our parents would not sit here together"

The Germans

Geb. 1945

Man hat uns gesagt
daß wir die Generation
der Stunde Null sind
Daraufhin habe ich
das Lexikon genommen
und nach der Null geschaut
Null – die Zahl
die zu einer anderen hinzugezählt
diese nicht verändert
a + 0 = a
Daraus folgt ferner
a x 0 = 0
Jedoch kann man eine Zahl
nicht ohne weiteres durch Null teilen
Die Null ist Sinnbild
der Nichtigkeit und
Bedeutungslosigkeit."
Nach diesem Zitat aus dem
Neuen Brockhaus
habe ich angefangen
ein Problem
meines Jahrgangs zu erfahren
Es ist – wie man sieht –
rein mathematischer Art!

Born 1945

They told us
that we are the generation
of the hour zero

So I took the dictionary
looking for zero
Zero – the number
when being added to another
doesn't change it
a + 0 = a
hence it follows
a x 0 = 0
however it is not possible
to divide a number by zero
zero is symbol
of being nothing and of
meaninglessness."
After this quotation from
New Brockhaus
I was beginning
to experience a problem
of my year of birth
it is – like is to be seen –
only of mathematical kind!

Sie sind ja eine andere Generation

Sie sind ja eine andere Generation
sagte die alte Dame freundlich lächelnd
denn sie hat Deutschland geliebt
Ich bin eine andere Generation
Ich spür ihre Hoffnung
fühl die Erwartung
und weiß nicht
was ich tun soll

You are another generation
the old lady said smiling friendly
for she had loved Germany
I am a different generation
I feel her hope
feel the expectation
and do not know
what to do

(Irmgard Dettbarn)

***

"Our liberation from National Socialism by the Allies took place in the spring of 1945. But '1945' in my world of that time meant the 'breakdown', not the 'new beginning'. I was 8 years old at the time, and still remember the boundless joy at my first chocolate bar from a black American, at my first rubber ball, at a dog and a cat, animals which followed us home and for which my family suddenly had room. The new persons in my neighborhood, the fugitives, came into my life almost as wordlessly as the others had gone before 1945. We called one man the 'Mayor of Silesia'. Why did they come to us? 'The Russians', was the answer, and to the present day there is still something hair-raising for me about countries in the 'East'. The world of the adults was dominated by rubble clearance after the war, by concerns about private, by everyday calls of nature and by the withdrawal of the Americans and their replacement by the English: as if the US conquerors had cheated us of true liberation by handing us over to the English" (Christoph Biermann).

***

"Last week on June 20, 2001, my father died at the age of 81. Since then I think even more than before that I am not personally responsible for what has happened. I knew this before, but now I think so even more. I presume that he was one of those horrible soldiers in the last war who killed everyone he

could, even those he just wanted out of the way – like mosquitoes bothering him. During my childhood I feared that he would kill me if I dare to say something about him that he didn't like to hear. This danger shadowed my life.
My father accused me of wishing to kill him.
I am glad that he died of illness and old age.
I did not kill him after all" (Irmgard Salzman).

***

"The Small Study Group confronted me with the discovery that I had used my knowledge of my parents' ideological (not political) opposition against Hitler and his system to defend myself against the possibility that my father had been involved in destructive action, against Jews, in particular, while serving as a soldier in Russia.

All of a sudden, I knew – and I have known since then – the strength of the defences which most Germans have built up against their involvement in National-Socialism and the Holocaust. If it applies to me, one of the children of the war – how much more does it apply to the generation of my parents. I guess that it was the atmosphere in the conference which was confrontational, but also full of respect for the other, which helped me to confront this insight. It is precisely this atmosphere which we find difficult to create in Germany where there is a constant need to prove our horror of and our distance to the destructiveness of the Holocaust among the liberal and left intellectuals" (Veronika Grueneisen).

***

"In this meeting with the Jewish-Israeli participants I had the experience how guilty and shameful it feels if I don't deny my origin: being a German.

How is it possible not to deny my origin and at the same time distant or even disidentify my inner self? To state that I hope, and am working on, not being like so many of my parents and grandparents generation? How can one be sure about it?

This uncertainty is what can allow for a German psychoanalytic identity – neither denying the parents guilt, or my own potential involvement, nor identifying with it" (Thea Wittmann).

***

"Eventually, however, we Germans will also have to mourn over the lost members of our country which have been severed. I firmly believe that we would be much less trustworthy if we continue to pretend that we do not care about that loss. It has a lot to do with feeling fragmented or whole – integrated. The strange thing is that I myself never even felt that something was missing when Germany was still divided into two separate states.

Yet when unification had taken place and was celebrated one evening in 1990 by an open air-concert with Leonard Bernstein conducting Beethoven's Ninth Symphony, I was quite surprised to suddenly have this feeling of wholeness. That experience taught me that with regard to my country I had previously only reacted on an intellectual level without ever mourning" (Armin Pollmann).

***

Womb

Dark and mysterious
the English word
the German practical
Gebärmutter
take it out,
and you will find
A way to live without
the thing
the mother
after having
given birth
to children
live with then
lead them to live
out of the dark
out of the blood
out of the tears
into the open

to the father
to words
to life
with tears
and blood
and wombs again
to give birth to children
and lead them
to live with the other
all the others
to find ways
to cope
to speak
to tell
of life and tears and blood and wombs again

blood

Blood
my om
mom
be alone bleeding
bloody
hopeless helpless muscle
perfidious bag
ashes
of motherhood
(Irmgard Salzmann)

***

"During the conference I found myself in a peculiar role, although experiencing myself as part of the German group, I also found myself an outsider, at the same time feeling I had an acute inside knowledge of the German mind set and experience. However, I also felt close and familiar with the experience of the Israeli participants, especially those of my Small Study group and others with whom I had opportunity to speak more personally. Since my experience in Bad Segeberg, I have come to formulate my perspective as one of being *an insider and outsider* to both sides, and of changing perspectives. As a result of my experiences as a German emigrant I have developed a rather more acute perception of German attitudes having had the opportunity to look at myself, my people, my culture from the outside. In addition I have also had the experience of looking at myself as a German through Jewish eyes. And I think in the process I have developed an awareness too of a Jewish perspective, the experience behind it, the presence of the trauma of the past within the Jewish communities and between Jews/Israelis and Germans. In this sense I feel that I have some inside knowledge of Jewish/Israeli experience of the presence of the past, at least I feel I have had more experience and opportunity to become aware than many other Germans. However, I also found during the conference that I can feel rather too critical, angry and impatient when I am confronted with certain German attitudes which I know too well from the past ...

What I found striking was the impression that the Israeli members of the group had a clear and strong sense of identity, which gave them a vitality in communicating who they were, what were and how strong their loyalty with their parents/grandparents and families as victims which the Germans in the group lacked. The majority of Germans had no and seemed unable to find a narrative about who they were, who their parents were, how they lived, felt, what they thought, what their experiences were. I felt this very acutely myself, and it is a typical feeling I have as a German meeting others in the international community.

Unless asked or introduced, it would never occur to me to want to tell someone who I am as this would reveal me as being German. It feels easier, more bearable to be no one, non existent that having to face the feelings connected with being German" (Hella Ehlers).

***

The Israelis

"My mother was born in Berlin, She sent me to 'The Deutsche Schule' in Montevideo. After high school and army I even wanted to meet the Germans and know them in their country. In the last years I have been more and more withdrawn from Germans and Germany. It was hard (in the Conference) for me to be in contact with the Germans, it felt like a betrayal, I could hardly speak German with them and that only from the 3rd day on. I had dreams where I saw the number on the hand of my aunt who raised me. I realized that the relations I had with my unit at the army during war stemmed from this source of mutual commitment, of never betraying" (Robi Friedman, letter to the editors).

***

"My father was born in Germany 1905, he left Germany January 1933, coming back to the hospital where he worked after Christmas holiday, he was informed he couldn't go on working there as a physician. His eldest brother left Germany earlier and moved to England with a German woman with whom he fell in love and married, no children.

I remember as a little girl asking my father endlessly what made him leave Germany and take his parents with him. He told me about his Zionist education in the youth movement 'Blau Weiss', but he never told me about the anti-Semitism he suffered from ...

Summer 2000, Bad Segeberg, plenary session, a beautiful German woman (Stereotype of the female SS in movies?) says: 'I have an ordinary Nazi mother.' The lake and the forest are so beautiful, the 'Appfle Kuchen', the Herring and the 'Kartofel Salad' are so tasty. I am in a small study group with a German consultant, always critical towards him, difficulty to accept German authority, and here comes an amazing thought – *I have an ordinary Nazi-Jewish mother! Me?*" (Daniela Cohen)

***

"But do I really want to? I don't 'feel like' coming (to Bad Segeberg). Too heavy. Once I see myself as an American (Jewish) soldier coming to this Nazi country in 1945, and once as a fearful Jew who tries to get lost unnoticed (during the war) otherwise he will be shot on the spot. I fear that I'll not be able to sleep all the nights there, and everyone will see how frightened I become, being on this land and not be able to distinguish between fantasy and reality. Or maybe, to put it better, between history and here-and-now reality. What is the reality anyway when a Jew is walking freely in Germany and yet there are still those who would rather wish him dead? But it is not a good enough argument because here (Middle East), we are not so welcomed too, and nevertheless I'm staying.

This was the first thought about Nazareth III in Germany. Now it is time for the second and the third" (Yoram Hazan).

***

"My childhood was connected chronologically to the war in Europe and went with me always: on the one hand the magic of the German culture through the music, literature and the views that I don't know but imagine through books, on the other hand the horror of the German-Nazi reality. I was born at the same year that Hitler rose to power, in a country far away from Europe, yet all my life was dictated by what happened there, as a Jewish person and as an professiona" (Pnina Weisman-Zahor).

***

The Israelis through German Eyes

"Saturday evening, the fourth evening of the conference, Sabbath for the Israelis, I join some colleagues for a stroll to Bad Segeberg. Some other participants, Israelis and/or Germans are supposed to be somewhere. In a restaurant we meet a group of 12 or 13 persons, a German colleague, a German with Jewish roots, the rest all Israelis, sitting around a table in the next room. I was invited to join them, and experienced this not as a polite empty invitation, I felt very welcome. It seemed almost as a move of the group that opened to take me in. I felt: today this is my place.

In the course of the evening two or three times other colleagues joined the group shortly, and I was again able to feel this kind of move: a full heart hallo, not just shifting of chairs or inviting gestures.

Is it an expression of Israeli mentality, a Mediterranean way of life? Or are these descendants of families of which so many were murdered, that

always there are many free places – like wounds – for newly arriving persons?
I had taken the last free chair and was curious and happy, felt welcome" (Thea Wittmann).

***

The missing/missed "Jews"

"I remember my own initial ambivalence when I found this was happening (Having the German members who were also Jewish): on the one hand: an irritation that our neat boundaries had been breached and on the other hand a feeling of delight that this was going to throw in something new and fascinating light that we had not bargained for. It does seem to have been a great success from that point of view" (Eric Miller).

***

"It is somehow strange that in a conference which focuses on the Shoah and its effect on the present, the word 'Jew' does not figure. A psychoanalyst would immediately think that this is due partially to the fact that the German word for Jew, 'Jude' has unbearable connotations connected with the extreme traumatic experience and hid memories of the Holocaust (annihilation, extermination, humiliation). Clinical practice has taught us how counterproductive it can be to confront a patient during treatment with words which can release unbearable states of mind. Particularly in the case of severe traumatized Patients, one would always be careful about using words whose traumatic context might re-traumatize the patient.

Seen in this light, the absence of the word Jew in the title of this conference may well be understood as an attempt to keep the emotions that could be sparked off through the confrontation with this theme at a bearable level. This is in spite of the fact that the title is in English and that the word 'Jew' would not necessarily arouse the same feelings as the German word 'Jude'.

Nevertheless, I ask myself if the absence of the word 'Jew' in the title might not have other implications. Are we only looking at the absence of a word?

In this connection I cannot help but ask myself the following:
Does avoiding the word 'Jew' in the title in fact indicate something else?
The existence of the state of Israel safeguards the continuity of a Jewish identity the existence of which was threatened by the Nazi genocide. Jews in the Diaspora establish and preserve the Jewish identity out of Israel.

Some of us live in Germany. We find ourselves confronted daily with the theme of the Holocaust, because of 'our' history and because of the German history. We speak about it (or remain silent about it) with our German pupils, teachers, friends and patients.

We seem, though, not to be expected, in a conference which is called: 'Germans and Israelis: The Past in the Present'.

The following questions remain unanswered:
1. Is a dialogue between Germans and Jews possible as long as the word 'Jew' with all its emotional implications must be avoided in the title of the conference?
2. Is the avoidance of the word 'Jew' in the title a form of assault on the Jewish identity? Is it not a denial of an existing part of the Jewish identity, the Diaspora Jews?
3. Is it possible that an identification with the aggressor takes place which causes the word 'Jew' to be seen as a word to be avoided at all costs?
4. Are not past humiliations of the Jews being projected on the Diaspora Jews and in particular on the Jews living in Germany? Do they become representatives of the unwanted, humiliated Jew?
5. Does the avoidance of the word 'Jew' in the title of this conference indicate that part of the Jewish identity is left away, because it represents an unwanted, hated aspect of the Jewish 'personality', denied both by Germans and by Jews (Israelis)?

As I (a German Jew) nevertheless attended the first conference (Nazareth, June 1994) I felt out of place. I decided not to attend the following conferences" (Laura Viviana Strauss).

***

"Before the conference, in 1999, Shmuel Erlich saw a need for an open letter in the 'Psyche' to his Jewish colleagues in Germany to provide them with an extra invitation. This was not successful. I don't know anything about the possible unconscious fantasies being also part of these processes, and I don't know who those colleagues were that did not want to get together at the conference. But, we should presume they had important reasons for not doing so. A Jewish colleague from Germany, who did not attend the conference, drew my attention to the fact that we, the non-Jewish Germans could never know for sure who amongst the Germans at the conference were Jewish. 'A Jew does not always think this should be something he wants to speak about,' he said. I suppose that this kind of holding back comes from expectations or even experiences like that incident in the Conference in which a Jewish colleague from Germany was a little late for her small study group and was greeted unexpectedly by a non-Jewish German with the words: 'I thought you had committed suicide.'

Maybe the Jewish colleagues from Germany did not want to join because they did not feel safe in the presence of us, the non-Jewish Germans. If this is true, it provides a motive for thinking about it. Maybe both sides are still not ready to talk about — not even to another – the past in the present?" (Eva-Maria Staudinger)

***

"TO THE EDITOR of the PSYCHE: The Plight of Jews in Germany

I am moved to address this difficult issue by my professional connection and personal experience with a special kind of Working Conference, *'Germans and Israelis: The Past in the Present'*, about which I shall have more to say presently. But I am also doing so out of my own personal life history and identity, which, in many ways, ties me closely with this painful point. Being born in Frankfurt a/M in 1937, my family – parents, older sister and I – lived through the terrible events and persecution that culminated in Kristallnacht and our escape from Germany, to what was to become Israel, in December 1938. I was raised in a home atmosphere through which I experienced, on an almost daily basis, the pain of having been torn, expelled and vomited as unwanted by a culture and language that was nonetheless an unchanging part of my parents' identity, and through them, of my own. In my formative years, I was never physically a 'Jew in Germany,' yet most of the time very much a 'German Jew'. I came back to Germany for the first time on my 40th birthday, and numerous times since then. Each and every time I have had the uncanny experience of being 'back home', and at the same time – of being a total stranger and outsider, very much wanted or barely tolerated, as the case may be.

I may be projecting my own experience on others, but I have good reason to believe that my experience speaks in more ways than one to many of the Jews who live in Germany today. Here I have in mind particularly those Jewish colleagues who share my psychoanalytic identity. Beyond the vicissitudes of personal histories and life stories, I have the strong feeling that they also share my own 'uncanny' experience of being at home while being strangely homeless, even today, in Germany. I do not question their decision to live there and to have to struggle with this experience. I do wish to inform them, however, that their personal plight is not unnoticed or unknown, to me as well as to many others.

The importance of publicly sharing this feeling, as well as the conviction this requires, come to me from taking part in two Working Conferences, in 1994 and 1996, in Nazareth, Israel. These conferences, *'Germans and Israelis: The Past in the Present'*, were attended by German and Israeli psychoanalysts and psychotherapists, and sponsored by the DPV and DPG, and IPS (Israel Psychoanalytic Society) and IPA (Israel Association of Psychotherapy). They were in the format of specifically adapted Group Relations Conferences, in the tradition of the Tavistock Institute of London. They were held under the professional auspices of OFEK – Person, Group, Organization – The Israel Association for the Study of Group and Organizational Processes, and the academic and organizational auspices of The Sigmund Freud Center of The Hebrew University of Jerusalem. The special design of the conference recognized the two national groups – Germans and Israeli/Jewish – as the starting point for understanding and exploring the group and individual processes, rational and irrational, covert and overt, conscious and unconscious.

In a way that could not have been anticipated, the complexity of Jewish identity emerged powerfully, profoundly, and often in a personally painful manner, in both these conferences. It became convincingly clear that various participants held within themselves and their personal identities the conflicted and even tormented part of being a 'Jew in Germany', perhaps of being a 'Jew-in-conjunction-with' yet other identity component. The experience of this finding was enormously instructive and helpful, but also difficult and uneasy. It is in many ways particularly unnerving for some of us Israelis to find this complicated Jewish identity within ourselves, having tried to disavow it in favor of a newly born and liberated Israeli identity. What is so hard to bear is precisely the uncanny experience that I referred to: It means to be both 'in' and 'out', to belong and yet not to be a part of the group, at one and the same time. The experience can be closely and uncomfortably akin to madness.

I think and believe, however, that these conferences are important precisely because they can help us encounter experiences of this kind. It is important to take part in them, if we wish to learn, through our own experience, what it means to be German or Jewish or Israeli in the post-Holocaust age we live in. It means that the plight of being 'a Jew in Germany' is not merely an isolated personal fate. It has meaning and significance at the level of the group and the wider intra- and inter-national sphere of existence. It cannot be overestimated or overstated how valuable for our work as psychoanalysts and psychotherapists it is to come to grips with such issues *in the presence of the other*, which alone make it possible to do this work. It is of great value for us Israelis to have Jews who live in Germany take part in this, as much as it is for Germans to have both Jews and Israelis present in order to carry out their own difficult work. Neither one of these groups can do so without the others. Perhaps this is even more crucially important for the next planned Working Conference, which will take place for the first time in Germany.

I hope that bringing these thoughts and experiences to the attention of readers in Germany will contribute to the recognition of the work already done by these conferences and of the great potential they still hold for all of us" (H. Shmuel Erlich).

***

"In the third meeting of the Small Study Group I tried to say why I am here. It is hard to talk about. I am looking for something that is missing. How can I express the feeling that I am missing the Jewish way of life, the Jewish people? Does a feeling like this have a right of existence?

I read about the former Jewish life in Germany. Repeatedly I read about 'Gefillte Fish'. How does it taste? How does it smell? What was the atmosphere when it was prepared? I don't even know if I would like to eat it – I know that there once was something which now doesn't exist any more, and I miss that something. I can feel it now" (Thea Wittmann).

※※※

IV.3   The Conferences Experience

"I am so disappointed – why are there so few Israelis here?" This question of a German analyst opened the first Nazareth Conference. An immediate answer came from an elderly Israeli woman: "If you had not killed so many of us, there would have been more here." This dialogue set an understated as well as a "no-nonsense" tone to this conference as well as to the following ones. Participants came to the conference with trepidations: the days ahead of then will not be easy, the decision to come to this conference was not easy to begin with.

At the third conference we learned that it took some members 4 years of deliberation to attend the conference.

In the psychoanalytic community in Germany the knowledge and interest in the Conferences was well spread due to considerable work that has been done by the German initiators. Following each conference, participants in Germany presented their experience to their professional communities, a process that is still ongoing. For many potential members these presentations started an inner dialogue that was actualized in participation in a following conference. For many others this inner dialogue is still going on.

It is not easy to be a member in these conferences, neither is it to be on staff for that matter (an issue that will be dealt with later). Participants came to do an important internal work in the presence of the "Sames" and the "Others". Painful moments were the order of the day, but so were moments of deep sorrow and compassion.

※※※

The Long way to the Conference

"I can imagine somebody who asks me if it is worthwhile to participate in a further conference. My answer would be: there is absolutely no question, you must participate!

But – you must be aware of some dangers.

You might have read a lot about the Holocaust and you think you know a lot of these matters. Yet suddenly you feel a certain anxiety, sometimes that only your body can tells you.

Some of us got ill. Some of us decided before head to be brave. Some did not tell that they are going to the conference, because they did not want to justify themselves. Most of us have small circles of friends and only there they want to speak about their feelings.

Suddenly the world is divided in to those who accept this topic and those who do not. And you don't want to hear again and again that we are fed up with this subject in Germany, more than 50 years after the Holocaust.

And you notice that you can't help wondering: 'what did your father do when he was a teacher in the forties?' or: 'what do *you* know about your father and mother?'

But why this question!? It is their history, and it's past.

Then the conference begins and suddenly the past is present. You feel that you are looked at as a German, perhaps even as a Nazi? You want to reassure the Israelis that there is no danger: they will be safe if they go for a walk. But can you be sure that these old men there down at the lake have not been involved in the Holocaust? And you hope that there will be no Neo-Nazis near the lake.

You feel deeply ashamed about what your parents have done, about what happens in Germany today.

Some people may ask you before the conference to tell them about it afterwards. But then suddenly nobody wants to know. And you too might not want to reveal your inner feelings.

If you are lucky, you have some friends, but don't be disappointed if not.

Participating in such a conference is like a walk in the mountains: there are beautiful moments and dangerous parts and afterwards everybody tells another story, what impressed him or her most. You may be astonished of how deep precipices are trivialized afterwards" (Eva Mack).

***

"The decision to participate in the Conference was not an easy one. On one side I knew that I wanted to participate, because for years I have been committed to my therapeutic work with children of survivors. Therefore I though that such an experience would enhance my understanding of these patients and of myself as their therapist. On the other side I felt the emergence of resistances in dealing with this encounter. I found out that the most powerful resistance came from my wish to keep my hatred alive and my enemy focused, clear and unchanged. It was one of the ways to remember the Holocaust and not to feel a traitor to my people and my family. Moreover, I could sense that in some ways the feeling of hatred gave me a sense of power that I found hard to renounce.

Thinking about this internal struggle helped me make the decision to participate, but I felt that I wanted to go with my hatred as a starting point in this encounter. I thought that if this hatred could not be allowed to be felt and expressed toward the German colleagues, the whole experience could become not authentic, a waste of time. I was frightened by the arousal of these powerful emotions, and my anxiety reached a peak just before the beginning of the Conference, when I had to meet all these people coming from Germany.

One of the main reasons that contributed to my decision to participate was a vague notion that started to take form in my mind. For years, in different experiences, including my personal analysis, and in my work with Israeli colleagues I had the need to talk about the Holocaust experiences and their impact on my family and myself as a child of survivors. I always felt some shame and guilt, especially when I sensed that others would not want, or would not be able to listen, and I felt overburdened by my need. This gave me a sense of not having legitimization and being always out of place. It occurred to me that it was the first time that I would have the opportunity to deal with these issues for a whole week without feeling out of place, and this added to my sense of expectation, and to my fears. Finally, the issue of the Holocaust would not only be allowed, it would be encouraged.

Another important element that was present in the Conference was the fact that this was an encounter with 'The Enemy'. I have participated in workshops where children of survivors meet with each other to talk and work through experiences and memories, but it always left me with a sense of having participated in a process of mutual commiseration. Though legitimate, I didn't think it helped us 'to move on'. It left us 'stuck' in the same psychological places. Last but not least, the fact that the leaders of the group would be from different countries, with different perspectives, gave me a sense of security and an expectation of a good container" (Irene Melnick).

***

"When I received the first information about the conference, I knew at once that I 'had' to attend. I had been wrestling with the question of the newly rising violence against Jews and foreigners in our country for quite some time. I am convinced that this phenomenon is an answer to increasing social and economic injustice and social insecurity in our country, especially after the break down of socialism in East Germany, Eastern Europe and the Soviet Union. Yet, I also believe that there may be some social delegation in this violence: I live in a society which largely denies its structural violence and tries to forget about its destructive racist past and, maybe, present. The violent adolescents and children remind us of both. I also have been wondering what might be my contribution, as citizen and psychoanalyst, to meet and/or prevent some of this present destructiveness.

Moreover, I had known the Human Relations Program of the Tavistock Institute, London, and I had known Eric Miller from a previous conference. I had appreciated the Tavistock approach to learning about organisations, and I imagined that the inter-group event could be very helpful for the difficult task of this conference for Germans and Israelis.

The setting and the intent to look for *the other within myself* (as an individual, but also as member of a group) proved to me to be both confrontational and supportive for the learning process" (Veronika Grueneisen).

***

"I think that 'The Kippa Event' (see page 84 et seqq.) was the first time that Germans and Israelis created a 'mixture' in which the aggressor was not only a 'German made' one; on the contrary – both active aggressors were Israelis. Something could be (or shall I say, should be) learned about current Israeli aggression, which of course has its roots in the traumatic past. Enactment of the aggression by changing roles – now the 'victim' can be the 'aggressor' – was the essence of the learning process. It is my impression that what enabled us to go deeper than the point we had reached in Nazareth I, was the fact that we all are Nazareth I veterans.

The next question is a clear outcome of the above: is it the right time to consider the possibility of Nazareth III in Germany? Do we have enough knowledge to go up to the Third Grade of our investigation?

I wrote to Carl Nedelmann that my first counter-phobic tendency is to say 'yes' before I'll regret. Then I'll be 'committed' to it and the ambivalence is as-if resolved. My schizoid tendency is to say politely that this time it is not for me. I had enough adventures in my life and I can save myself this one.

Then, coming back to my more courageous years, I remember that the whole point in combat is that you continue going on and raise your head under fire, only because someone near you did it before. Now it is your turn, and later he will see you rising up, which, in turn, will give him strength. This is the whole story. So, if the German participants did it by coming to Israel twice – (Rosemarie, Gisela, Carl, Christoph, Siegfried, Helmuth, Thomas, Rolf, and others that I know less) – I think that now it is my turn" (Yoram Hazan).

***

"Thinking of Nazareth II for me it was a long time like a dark misty cloud wrapping around the heart. I felt 'left hanging' in an unhappy and painful way, not free to think or even write about my experiences.

While writing this, the map I bought before the trip to Israel is lying next to me. Now as then an orientation maybe needed to counteract the pain caused by lack of inner orientation. This was one main theme in Nazareth II.

The first parapraxis, expression of miss-orientation, was that I booked the hotel in Jerusalem one night short and when I came it was booked completely. I contacted with no notice an old acquaintance who lives in a kibbutz in the north of Israel, near the Syrian border.

After the excursion to the kibbutz the next morning I took the bus to Nazareth. From the bus stop near the hotel I walked up the street with my suitcase, aware of the soldiers guarding the area. The hotel is beautifully settled, the sun is shining. In the hotel lounge the first person I met was a German colleague badly upset because he left his watch somewhere. His dismay makes me uncomfortable. It is too much in the way.

This night in the hotel room I cannot fall asleep, something is humming – the air conditioner? I can't locate it, finally the vibrating sounds are unbearable. I'm thinking: 'Tomorrow I have to be strong, ready for the group situation.' I think: 'In another country I would try to change rooms.'

It is 23.30, I walk to the reception. It's not easy to find another room; the hotel is fully booked still I get a room in a small bungalow. Did I overreact? Did the humming disturb me because I am mistreated in Israel? A punishment for being German or is it is a technical problem of the hotel?" (Thea Wittmann)

***

"The subject of the meeting has, as you know, occupied me for a long time. I think that you chose a very apt title for it.

I have a question with the methodology which was applied to it. I told you that I never had attended a Tavistock conference before and that I was therefore very eager to become a participant in Nazareth and an observer of its methods. From what I had heard about it I feared that the meeting might become a sort of public confessional and pseudo-analyses. This was fortunately not the case. On the other hand I did not feel that the promise of the title was reached beyond a superficial level. It was more or less a getting acquainted which might have been for many of the participants in a measure a first step forward. Yet with a few exceptions the past, (and not yet the most personal inner past as it related to the group past) was not touched upon in significant ways. Occasionally I had reason to be astonished at the ignorance of the actual history on both sides" (Martin Wangh).

***

"These are special conferences. A remark by a Jewish staff-member in Bad Segeberg can demonstrate some of this Specialness. The Jewish staff member said in a plenary: 'Our parents would not sit here together.'

Some parents did not even want to know to which kind of meeting their 'children' were on the way to, maybe because they feared to be betrayed there. A non-Jewish member from Germany as preparation for Bad Segeberg dared to ask her parents for the first time in her life – what did they do in the war-time. This question followed by a declaration of the parents that they no longer had a daughter – the past in the present. This conference was the first one in Germany. This made all the participants anxious, although the conscious, pre-conscious and unconscious sources of anxiety of course, have all been very different" (Eva-Maria Staudinger).

***

"You and the other editors asked especially for impressions from System Event. I hardly remember them, mainly my feeling of having been left by the consultant-'parents', and moreover of having been pushed into a madly aggressive situation by some of their interpretations, which often did not convince me. But this probably was intentional: to confront ourselves with the inner psychological forces. Mr. Miller said at the end of the conference: 'You are not here to feel comfortable' – and I think he was right.

Linked to this a more general remark: The main task of the conference as formulated in the invitation – 'to get into contact with ones' hatred' – *[This is of course a subjective reading of the Primary Task, which was: To provide opportunities for participants to explore how feelings and fantasies about 'German-ness' and 'Israeli-ness'/Jewish-ness influence relations within and between the two groups in the conference. MEG.]* makes sense. But is seems to me that it is somehow too narrow: we are not asked to get into contact with what we felt, and hatred might of course be an important part of it. I often experienced the consultants' interpretations – like in a misunderstood Kleinian version – as pinning us down to hatred, which in my opinion leaves aside a wide scale of feelings, the libidinous ones. What nevertheless was important for me in the System Event: After having gone through very painful confrontations finally there was more readiness for exchange" (Jutta Matzner-Eicke).

***

To Be in a Conference – How Does the Conference Work

"The Pain of Unbearable Guilt and Mourning is More Unbearable if Borne Alone."

The power of any Group Relations Conference is in the special combination of strong boundaries provided by the setting: working sessions start and end according to the designated timetable, the primary task of each event is the compass of the event, the staff stay in role in a clear and transparent way, all of this allows for the possibility of loosening the personal boundaries and for greater inner freedom to explore and meet the unknown. The group processes acts as an amplifier, while the setting contains the "unbearable". In the GIC conferences the group is composed of two main national groups which create a divide of: "our own kind" and "others". The meeting of these groups creates the juxtaposition, the conflict and the dialogue. Our claim is that this kind of work is possible only in this kind of group setting that holds within it the possibility not to be alone while bearing the "pain of unbearable guilt and mourning" as well as the actual presence of the "other".

The strong and clear boundaries of the conference serve as the container for the "unbearable" feelings, creating a potential space in which people are more regressed than their usual everyday selves: they are more sensitive to themselves, to others, and to the interface between inner and outer realities. This is the source of dreams, images and fantasies that are woven through the collective work into a tapestry of meaning.

It is unknown and unpredictable where the meaningful moments and processes for each member will be located. This fact is reflected in the contributions that relate meaningful moments from different events: for some it was the intimacy of the Small Study Groups ("my Small-Study-group-family") that allowed it, for others it happened during the System Event. Some found the "unexpected" during the Plenaries, and for some the more defined Review and Application Groups turned out to be surprisingly meaningful. The following excerpts refer to the different events and give the feel of the intensity that prevailed throughout.

***

"This conference concerned itself with the attempt to deal with a new, unusual way of looking at the mutual history of Germany and the Jews in the period 1933 to 1945. New, because until now nothing like this has existed, that German and Israeli psychoanalysts and psychotherapists sit down together and speak with one another for a whole week over the special relationship between the Germans and the Jews. Unusual, because it should have been more – indeed was – more than a talk about the relationship; because based on the fundamentals of the Tavistock model, each participant should be able to learn about himself by his personal conflict which he had in the discussions about the past with differently perceived Israeli and German analysts.

The aspect that especially interested me at this conference has something to do with the reviving of our German past within the happenings of a large group. It is mentioned again and again that the past casts its shadows and has an impact on the present, yet how does it manifest in the every day life?

I myself know from discussions with colleagues the expectation that one must, as a German and especially as a German psychoanalyst, identify with the culprits if one desires to deal with working out the Nazi past. The people who required this at that time, unfortunately, never indicated how they themselves managed to identify with the side of the culprits.

In Nazareth, it was made possible in the increasing regression, group processes could unfold which illuminated something of that which must have happened in Nazi Germany when groups came together: an emotionality with increasingly dangerous undertones and an increasing suspension of rationality. Those who could, as participants at Nazareth, allow that such an atmosphere will plant itself within oneself and those who had enough confidence in the supportive functions of setting, staff and other group members, could enrich one's psyche by a strongly suppressed aspect of one's social existence" (Angelika Zitzelsberger-Schlez).

***

"Allowing these destructive and painful fantasies and feelings, sharing them with others *and* also conveying them to Jews, is very far-reaching for a process of coming to terms between Germans and Israelis and presupposes a high degree of trust in the protective resources and good internal self-and object representations. At the same time, this group scene is only possible if the group works on a basis that is primarily personal-individual and 'humane', and the trauma of the Holocaust, especially the experience of the Israeli participants, is only present to a limited extent. Otherwise an overwhelming degree of anxiety, hate and revenge would presumably take shape on the Israelis' part and the Germans would no longer be able to tolerate the extent of their fear of revenge and the extent of their own feelings of guilt and shame. But in this way, on the basis of primarily 'individual' work, far-reaching identifications with the 'Nazi poison', the 'ugly German', were possible on the Germans' part, e.g., even when the German and Jewish participants of one System Event group tried to get at the possible fascination of Nazi songs and a German (female) participant sang the 'Horst Wessel song'" (Ursula Kreuzer-Haustein).

***

Fascination
They want to hear
Hitler songs
don't they know
the poison
they take in
did nobody
warn them
against
catchy tunes
(Irmgard Salzmann)

***

"I needed the other in a controlled psychotherapeutic work-situation to help me to identify and separate fantasies-prejudices and facts from actual experiences arising in the encounter. I didn't know that the past is still so powerful in the present as I experienced it in the first conference in which I found myself repeating symbolically the perpetrator trauma of my parents in being part of the German group which 'abolished' the Israeli group because of a 'dirty fight' among the two German subgroups DPG and DPV about who's psychoanalysis is the 'true' one.

For my way out of my neurotic problems it seems as if I have to go back to real historical actions of my parents in the presence of victims of the second generation. I have to find out how much it effected me: dominating everything else The 'silent chimera-monster', a clinical syndrome of elicitability of strong psychic forces of 'different origin, sticking together, under a cover of silence in split off normal' daily life for the German group. This showed up in our two-group encounter" (Thomas Erdmann).

***

"I cannot emphasize enough how unique and different it has been to work on and in this conference. It felt entirely different for me than any other Group Relations conference I had worked in. The modes of taking up one's professional role and responsibilities were colored by these differences. My colleagues and I felt a sense of mission, of contributing and being part of an endeavor of historical and social significance that reaches far beyond the immediate. There was also a strong feeling of camaraderie, even identification, with the members, and envy of *their* being privileged to be in the member's role. Part of me, and I know this to be true of other staff as well, would have preferred to be a member and not staff in this conference. This identification with members, who are also professional colleagues and often friends, makes it difficult to work with them without being either too close or too distant. The SSGs consultants reviewed the way they took up their role in this conference, which felt very different from the usual. We found the preferred stance was on the boundary between a 'Group Relations' and a 'facilitation' mode, at times even on the boundary of 'group psychotherapy.' We accepted the working definition of our role to be: *Partnership in Search of Understanding*" (H. Shmuel Erlich).

***

"It is impossible to describe the endless experiences emerging from so many hours of being together with ourselves and with other Israeli and German colleagues, but I will try to make some abstractions on what I thought was happening at a group level. Emotionally, the impact of the encounter was very strong, and it took many months of digesting in order to have some distance from it and be able to reflect upon it in a more detached way.

The first idea that I had, already during the Conference, was that we were entering in a way a world of psychological simulation. In order to clarify this point, I will use Judith Kestenberg's concept of 'reality transposition'. She says that children of survivors live in a dual world, that of the present and that of the parent's past. The past of the parents is organized into the present reality of the child. I already had sensed that my need to talk about the Holocaust, and the feeling of discomfort aroused by this need, had to do with this idea of the transposition organization of reality. In the conference, at least three levels of psychological reality were coming together for the participants.

1. The reality of being a professional participating in a Tavistock oriented group, in order to experience, learn and think together about group processes.
2. The reality of being Jews and Germans, fifty years after the War, all of us trying to deal with the legacy of our parents and our peoples.
3. The psychological reality that 'we' were Jews in the concentration camps, and 'they' were the perpetrators, the Nazis.

The first two correspond to the present reality of our lives, the third belongs to the past and it emerges as a reality of the present. The group members and leaders had to hold these three psychological realities all the time in order to allow for the powerful emotional experiences to emerge and be dealt with by a 'sane' ego at the same time. The capacity to be in the present and in the past at the same time allowed us to make of this event a meaningful experience. The capacity to connect with the first two realities allowed us to simulate, 'to play' if you wish in the Winnicottian sense, to 'regress', to be 'crazy'. It was when connected with this level of reality that powerful emotions were felt and expressed, such as hatred, guilt and shame" (Irene Melnick).

***

Work in the Presence of the "Other"

"Like traveling somewhere that no one has been before us, with the only possible partners to be with there."

Work in the presence of the Other is one of the most important facets and probably the unique contribution of the conference: the work that is done, and can only be done in the presence of the other. In a certain way, all the different contributions could be brought together under this heading.

This "other" (the Germans for the Israelis, the Israelis for the Germans) is a partner, perhaps the only possible partner, and yet also the strangest possible partner: The one who holds the opposite pole, symbolizing (belonging) to the perpetrators/victims side. To use Primo Levi's image: the two who find themselves in the same trap, yet one of them did conceive and prepare the trap.

Why is it so important to have the presence of this "other"? Can't we just be among "ourselves" – those who share the common fate, those who are on the same side? This is the rationale behind different Support Groups. We believe that to do the personal inner work needed in order to get out from the imprisonment of the past, the actual presence of the "other" is a necessary though not sufficient condition. The presence of one's own group provides a mirror for looking at one self and exploring the variety of feelings towards one's own group.

The "other" in the conferences offers himself to be used so as to check projections – persecutory, idealizing and others – and to transform them into relationships. It is this work, which happens on the boundary between the inner world and outer reality, that contributes to the power of the conference.

The past in the present

Germans and Israelis

So many ...

So many deaths
No corpses
So many corpses
No funeral

So many funerals
No mourner
So many mourners
No comfort

So little comfort
So much guilt
So much guilt
So little justice

So little justice
So much hurt
So many hurts
No feeling

So many feelings
No word
So many words
So much silence

So much silence
No life
So many lives
No chance

So many chances
never taken.
(Irmgard Dettbarn)

***

"In my Small Study Group I witness a situation that for me was nearly unbearable: an attack by an Israeli on a German participant.

The German member spoke about his father, about his new ability to ask his father about his Nazi past, to listen to him – this was for him possible only after his participation in Nazareth I. A short time after this conversation with his father, his father died.

The sadness and mourning of the German for his recently deceased father was unbearable for the Israeli participant, whose own parents and relatives were killed by Nazis. It seemed as if there was no common space for the descendents of the second generation; the children of the culprits and the children of the victims, with their inner objects, their grief, and the transmitted and accepted obligations of loyalty.

It was unthinkable for me even after the group session was over to comfort or show compassion to a German participant who obviously was hurt; I didn't even think of it. I reacted in the same way that was described as the 'mode of Nazareth I': the lack of support between German members. Everyone is on his own, maybe even glad if pain affects another one and not on oneself.

My experience of the Jewish colleagues was that they showed their concern for each other openly. Even when aggressive to each other it was clear that underneath there was a connection, perhaps a connection against us, the Germans.

Perhaps we, the Germans, instinctively avoided everything that gave the appearance of a big German group. Perhaps each one of us felt it safer to avoid being thought of as guilty, of being part of a collective.

To give room to the experience of grief by the Israelis and to our grief as Germans, is to face the Nazi cruelties and the many dead, as well as our (German) latent inability to mourn. Maybe this is a dream. In Nazareth II it was not to happen" (Thea Wittmann).

***

"The theme of hate/fascination, guilt and guilt processing was linked to another issue: Is it even worthwhile and 'legitimate' for Germans, in the presence of Israelis, to articulate their hatred for the Nazi fathers and for being entangled in guilt feelings? Above all at the beginning of the conference, a few Germans were exceptionally scrupulous about even 'taking up room'. It was a matter of guilt and mourning exhibitionism, which seemed unnecessary to the Israelis and was a burden for them. If anything, the constant doubts and scruples about what we as Germans should even be allowed to get out of something merely paralyze the hatred and the accusations of the victims. As this reticence on the Germans' part was gradually overcome, a few German colleagues in the small groups dealt with the uncertain question about the extent of their fathers' involvement in Fascism. Interestingly, it was hardly a matter of the mothers. There were extremely painful reports accompanied by intense feelings of sorrow and hate on the part of a few individual Germans about real or fantasized crimes of their fathers, which some Israelis followed with interest and empathy. An image took shape in which both, Israelis and Germans, could mourn in the same house, but in separate rooms" (Ursula Kreuzer-Haustein).

***

The Kippa Event

"In the middle of Sabbath lunch time, one of the German members puts on his head a Kippa. An Israeli who sits at the same table, gets mad at him because he hates 'all orthodox Jews; they suppress us, the secular Jews'. So, he gets angry saying that he will kill all the orthodox Jews. A religious member-woman wonders, 'Do you want to kill all the people who have a Kippa just because of that? You don't know what their political views are! They might be leftist as you and me too.' He continues to be very aggressive, 'I don't care'. Another Israeli gets mad at the first one, saying to him: 'If I'll see you killing him (the German with the Kippa), I'll kill you'.
I found myself
1. defending someone who has a Kippa on his head
2. defending a German member
3. being extremely aggressive towards a compatriot, 'one of my own kind'.

I got not a few 'cold showers' from my Israeli friends and it took more than few minutes to make it clear to my 'attackers' that I will fight for this democracy and I'll not allow someone to be in a position to kill 'the other' just because he wore a Kippa and this makes someone mad at him. If 'there and then' in 1933, were some crazy people who would kill the one who already started to kill 'the others', history would be different.

To understand what is going on here now, we have to grasp something that happened 'there and then'. For that we need a partner with whom it will be possible to touch the bedrock of the experience. There is no way to touch the bedrock without being in contact with our inner Nazi 'part' and try to understand how it was to be a citizen in Germany in those times, how difficult it was to think, not to say – to stand up against. Only by that we can probably stop the danger of Fascism here.

I think that 'The Kippa Event' was the first time that Germans and Israelis created a 'mixture' in which the aggressor was not only a 'Germany made' one; on the contrary – both active aggressors were Israelis. Something could be (or shall I say, should be) learnt about current Israeli aggression, which of course has its roots in the traumatic past. Enactment of the aggression by changing roles – now the 'victim' can be the 'aggressor' – was the essence of the learning process. It is my impression that what enabled us to go deeper than the point we had reached in Nazareth I, was the fact that we all were Nazareth I veterans" (Yoram Hazan).

***

"Toward the end of the Second Nazareth Conference, one German member was a target of massive hostility because he had put on a Jewish prayer cap, a Kippa, on the Sabbath. He was asked in the plenary why he had done that. He remained silent. 'That's like German soldiers making fun of pious Jews', they said. 'He should justify why he, a German, put on a Kippa. That's blasphemy', they said. He remained silent. An enormous accusative tension that existed in both groups was unleashed against him, a form of hate. Later we learned that he did not want to reply at first because he wanted to protect something precious that was his own, but then he couldn't talk about it anymore, mute. Hidden behind the accusative tension, the hatred, there must be guilt, shame, anxiety and outrage that had not been accepted. They had to be noticed and accepted" (Hermann Beland).

***

"The fact that, almost incidentally, the subject of the history of the DPV and DPG also led to further alleviation of tension between the members of the two societies has something to do with the Israeli colleagues' interest in this history. They want to know why we have two societies. By telling them about it, we develop several versions together and finally come to speak about the 'prehistory', the time prior to the split: Eitingon, Jewish psychoanalyst and chairman of the first analytic institute in Germany, was driven out by the non-Jewish German colleagues and went to Israel. Perhaps, as one of the fantasies in the group has it, we were also coming together in Israel to see that he and his great-grandchildren, who are now living and working there, have survived" (Ursula Kreuzer-Haustein).

***

"Where to go from where we had to leave 'things'? Is there life to be found in the past or once the past returns in the present? I felt there is a danger, the experience of death is felt to be so enormous, overwhelming, it can leave us paralyzed, and we loose our mind and become speechless. I always think of this feeling in what Bion described as 'nameless dread'. But there is hope, and this is what seems to be bringing us together. As a German I felt that hope is regained in the presence of the Israeli group. The Israeli participants come to represent life, contradict the unconscious all are dead, existing in the German psyche as the unconscious fantasy of the extermination policy of the Nazi Germany. The presence of the Israelis disproves this, bringing us back to reality in the present: some have survived and there is something very alive to care about in the present" (Hella Ehlers).

***

"During an informal conversation with an Israeli, I experienced an unexpected feedback from my conversation partner. He called my attention to a nuance in my language in which I formulated my comments with conscious, emphatic philosemitism, but at the same time unconsciously used an expression with anti-Semitic associations. I had namely tried to 'respectfully emphasize', so to speak, the multicultural life story of my conversation partner; in the process the fact of his Jewishness, to my embarrassment, had come only at the end of my little list of the cultural spheres which distinguished him. As if that were not enough, I then tried to gloss over this awkwardness by letting the little phrase 'to boot' sneak into my following remarks, so that I ended by declaring: 'And then, of course, you are a Jew to boot.' His feedback left me with feelings of shame and confusion. As he spoke, however, the Israeli laid his hand on my arm, and this proximity helped bring clarity into my thoughts about the relationship between this situation and the topic of Anti-Semitism. We had both taken part previously on the small group session just mentioned. In the System

Event group, understandably, such a closeness of understanding in mutual interactions was missing.

Since this experience, it has become even clearer to me that anti-Semitism is actually a primary problem of anti-Semites, and that I as a German very likely need someone Jewish to talk to in order truly and authentically, if necessary, to recognize my own hang to anti-Semitism in the context of a German and Christian culture – that is, for example, in the medium of my own language. It has naturally disturbed me now for a long time when I read the words 'liquidation' and 'liquidate' on the bills of German physicians and therapists. My own formulation in this regard has always distanced itself from this – even if in a somewhat forced manner; for in thinking of that I actually go farther than I myself am aware of.

I see in this apparently naive German-collective linguistic behavior the trace of a 'basic assumption' in Bion's sense, one which set the tone in Nazism and which I have named 'interrelational arbitrariness' (C. Biermann 1995a). In outline, this basic assumption in this context can be formulated as follows: 'We Germans prefer to decide for ourselves what anti-Semitism concretely means among ourselves in the here and now. If Israelis and Jews express opinions about us in this regard, we take it as an expression of their – I might add understandable and unavoidable – hypersensitivity after the Holocaust.' I now wish in the following to use this formulation to describe the borderline situation on the part of German participants in that small group session which took up anti-Semitism as a 'system event' during the Nazareth II Conference. A bit of German 'interrelational arbitrariness' blocked progress in an understanding of anti-Semitism between Israelis and Germans and among the Germans themselves" (Christoph Biermann).

***

"My own edge-experience, the edge of that which I think I am able to bear, – seems pretty unspectacular. In the Small Study Group I helped someone, a German, with translating. And I said, what meant to be the helpful words: 'You are sitting in line.'

That moment, by chance, my eye rested on an Israeli colleague who seemed to collapse in front of my eyes. In my remembrance of that moment, it was misery; an accusation broke out against me, 'You seemed to be so friendly, but ...' It seems that my words showed my Antisemitism ('in line' is an often used expression to describe the queuing up of the Jews for extermination, Instantly I felt unspeakably guilty, not that I understood all neither of the Israeli colleague's words, nor at first understood at all what it was about. But, I had seen his immense pain and hurt, and, this in a colleague who just before had seemed to becoming more relaxed.

I was unable to offer resistance to his (and my own) overwhelming reaction; I became paralyzed and fell to tears. I just felt guilty. All of a sudden old body-symptoms were present again. Helplessly I apologized after finding speech again. I think that my Jewish colleague, like myself, was suffering from the weight of the past in the present. It was impossible for me to measure up the incident, to differentiate, to distance myself. Next to the personal neurosis, which always permeates extreme situations, in Seeon (in July, 1996 where both German Psychoanalytic Societies conferences took place, an outcome of Nazareth I) I had experienced myself as a bystander, yet I proved here by the use of what was for me a neutral word, that in fact, I am guilty after all? Wasn't it clear now that I'd be capable of doing anything? I doubted my ability to discern my feelings this doubt was what gave great impact to my feeling of guilt" (Thea Wittmann).

***

"Several Israelis also spoke in these smaller groups about speech habits of the Germans in relation to the issue of antisemitism in the here-and-now situation of the conference. Time and again, they said, Germans tend naively to use words and expressions historically connected in one way or the other to the Shoah without noticing the connection, as if such expressions were self-evident. For Jews, on the other hand, such connections between words and the Shoah are just as often real and present in their feeling for language. The German participants, at first markedly taciturn about the topic of anti-Semitism, expressed astonishment at this Israeli thesis. Someone then suggested that different feelings for language must be assumed on the part of Israelis and Germans, based on the differences in their individual histories; the important thing then, it was said, was that both sides be clear in their own minds about these differences: the Israelis had no right to expect that the Germans, as if by telepathy, should hastily adapt to the Jewish feeling for language. For this reason, misunderstandings must often be expected during this first phase. However, this understandably open-minded vote for mutual tolerance of speech was unable to crystallize into a core of consensus. Why? The starting points were too diverse: The Israelis had a problem with the 'German language' and interpreted this problem as showing a lack of empathy on the part of the Germans for the world of Jewish life, i.e. as a sign of latent anti-Semitism. For the Germans, on the other hand, such a primary problem of language was nonexistent. They felt themselves overburdened by the Israelis and unfairly accused of anti-Semitism. Personal communication thus broke down under the collective conditions of Jewish-ness and German-ness in the here and now" (Christoph Biermann).

***

IV.4 Looking at the Invisible: The Unthought Known and the Unspeakable

There is a lot of the "known" in the German-Israeli encounter: entire libraries have been written on the subject, about the perpetrators and about the victims, about first, second and third generations. Our task is to go beyond the known. When the apparent is so obvious one has to look harder to get to the invisible. Fantasies, Dreams, Unknowns, Unthought-knowns, Unspoken, and Unspeakable are the sign-posts in this search.

In the processes that unfold, surprising insights occurs at the most unexpected moments. It may be through reflecting on "Why did I leave the group I was in?"; A dream that received specific meaning in the context of a Social Dreaming Matrix; A sentence that echoes and becomes the key to a closed door that produces a whole story: Known and Unknown at the same time – Unthought-known.

The conference touches deep layers of the personal as well as the group existence and identity. It provides the containing boundaries for the unexpected to be explored, reflected about and accepted. This is part of the commitment and work of looking at the imprisonment of the past. The secure boundaries provided the safety also for speaking the "politically incorrect", the known but unspeakable; to challenge the "sacred cows" of groups and individuals.

***

"But what should be the reason for wanting to see history in a different way while challenging a taboo? What makes one join an event which could be seen as 'obscene'? Longing is a strong motive. Beside this I suppose inner needs, which compels to realize the damage of identity and the damage to relationships. What lies in the unconscious is that which is not bearable. In which way do these conferences make bearable what is unbearable. Those who were initiating the conferences formulated it like this: '… the pain of unbearable guilt and mourning is more unbearable if borne alone.' It is thorough the chance to share, sometimes even when this is unimaginable. This is what the conferences give" (Eva-Maria Staudinger).

***

"Among the Israeli group there were from the beginning tensions concerning issues of belonging and loyalty. Some members of this group needed to pull the Israeli group to a psychological place where 'we the survivors' felt a deep hatred and unwillingness to contact the 'perpetrators'. At the beginning of the conference, this group of Israelis could not make differentiations or go beyond the idea that 'all Germans are Nazis'. Another part of the Israeli group was not willing to be 'crazy' or undifferentiated, and conflicts arose within the Israeli group, with issues that dealt with betrayal, narrow-mindedness and divided loyalties. Interestingly enough, despite this tension, the German group was presented with the illusion that Israelis were united and with no inner conflicts.

In the beginning of the group process, it seemed to me that the Israelis had an easier time than the German colleagues. It s much easier to be in the position of the justified blamer and aggressor that emerges from a sense of victimization than to be the blamed one that will never be forgiven no matter what. Even though the conference was held in Israel and some German colleagues expressed fears of being destroyed by the Israelis, the German group was forced to accept the projections of being the Nazi exterminators, and they carried the guilt, the shame, the cruelty, with no expectations to be forgiven.

As the group progressed from this state of undifferentiation and massive projections, it was harder and harder for the Israeli group to keep the hatred alive and well. People became people, personal stories were told by both sides and as much as our German colleagues felt sorrow, compassion ad horror for our stories, we discovered reluctantly that their experiences were also heartbreaking. Empathy for their suffering began to emerge in the Israeli group and the question remained what to do with our hatred. Is it useful or is it just a poison to our minds and to the minds of our children? With no hatred, how do we remember or prevent it from happening again? When these processes started happening it was suddenly much harder for the Israeli group. The legacy to the next generations emerged as an important content in many groups. The German group had to deal with issues of how to give their children a sense of pride in themselves, their ancestors and their country, when they felt ashamed guilty and unforgiven. The Israeli group had to deal with how to keep the memory of the Holocaust alive, without poisoning their children with terrible feelings of hatred and the inability to forgive. The issues are unresolved" (Irene Melnick).

***

"For several days, a very tormenting equation prevailed, the equation being: German = Nazi. Finally a German colleague proposed a statement. She spent the night before in a tremendous psychic pain until she struggled through to propose her statement. What I remember or made of it, is approximately this: 'We, the German members of this group, have to face the fact, that after what the Germans in the time of Nazism made themselves responsible of – the Holocaust – we can't expect to be recognized by the Israeli colleagues as individuals. This is how it is. But we would like to state, that we do not accept a generalized guilt, but only that guilt for which one is personally responsible for.'

I felt fundamentally relieved by this, with the simple consequence: 'I am not my father, but his daughter.' This insight was for me, a more or less adult person with some psychoanalytical experience, certainly not quite new. But from that time on I felt able to live it more determinedly.

Linked to this is a much more personal experience.

A German member of the staff had encouraged me to go to Nazareth I with a kind of promise that after all, at the end one would feel recognized as a whole person and not be judged as a member of a group. This was a moving perspective – but I could not really believe it, mostly because of a tormenting discovery just before going to this conference: In a publication of my deceased Jewish analyst, whose sufferance during the time of Nazism I knew rather well, I found myself used as a case material, hardly made anonymous and very susceptible to be identified by colleagues. He described me as the subtly anti-Semitic child of an entangled, deeply conservative family who was overactive in the movement of 68, of course for the sake of manic defense. On the whole, this was true. But what was so painful to see was the misuse of my and my father's biography with a lot of aggravated and even false important facts. This description was impregnated with hate, my analyst could not have listened with goodwill, his countertransference had broken through. (I should like to add that on the whole I feel very grateful to him in retrospective).

With this in mind, I armed myself rather rigidly when coming to Nazareth. The way the consultant reacted to this in a small group was so moving and provided me with really new experiences: You made a remark about my cut-off state of mind and you reacted objectively and benevolently when I told the mentioned event with my analyst that until then was encapsulated inside me. This opened floodgates; and more important: This was a personal encounter, by which it was a bit more possible for me to get out of my entanglements and projections.

But I think my experience with my psychoanalyst is only a condensation of a much more general dilemma: We, Germans, cannot expect a Jew who suffered immensely to be a benevolent 'container' – he probably is not capable of it, when the person working with him, through his or her mere existence must remind him of his sufferings. But it is true and a psychoanalytical truism, that one needs just this benevolent container to get into contact with one's own personal guilt and entanglement" (Jutta Matzner-Eicke).

***

"There were coherent fragments, e.g. a German member expressing her personal dilemma: having grown up as child of parents who had loved her, but knowing that as pediatricians they may have known or even been involved in the *euthanasia program* (the systematic killing of mentally ill and disabled children and adults, which went on before applying this method of extermination to the 'Final Solution of the Jewish problem'). She still felt she has had loving parents. This was a chilling moment. But perhaps it gave us some clue for some of unspeakable feelings we felt in the group and were paralyzed by them without being able to name them. We thought we have been poisoned in the process of growing up in Germany. Later we thought of poems, Schubert's Winterreise. There was sadness in the group, which was beyond words. A feeling of something very precious lost, but remembered in the here and now between us" (Hella Ehlers).

***

"Small Study Groups are composed of 9–12 members of *both* nationality groups meeting with a consultant. Language and its powerful, preconscious way of surfacing unconscious and buried issues became an immediate focus. 'Innocent' words, as on the building floor plan, were loaded with meaning: 'Lager' (concentration camp), and 'Gruppenraum', which connected with 'Lebensraum'. The German environment was suffused with its cultural symbols and overtones. For some Israelis it was painfully connected with smells and tastes of food and cooking, trees and plants, and aspects of the physical surroundings – the sharp, unexpected surfacing of deeply missed childhood smells and tastes.

The immediacy of so many forgotten, forbidden and repressed memories made it difficult at first to speak in the Small Group. People spoke in hushed tones, in almost inaudible whispers – as in a house of mourning. No names were given or asked for. This changed suddenly when an Israeli woman said: 'I am named Sara, after my grandmother.' She and the group experienced this simple 'ordinary' statement as a bomb dropped in the room.

Another scene: All the women are dressed in black. Members are all mixed, surrounded by each other's nationality. Death and mourning are in the air, as well as the wish to let go of the burden of one's national identity. The manifest theme is *poison* and *paranoia*: being betrayed by one's parents; the world is a sick, cancerous place. The latent danger, however, is – shifts and changes in one's identity. The discussion turns to snow and winter. The consultant offers the association of Schubert's 'Gefrorene Traenen' ('Frozen Tears'). Dead parts of selves are buried under the snow, perhaps still alive. The question is, were the Israelis brought to Germany to thaw out the frozen German parts?

In the last session, members sit in same-nationality pairs. Again, they talk in hushed voices, as if in the presence of the dead. It is as if the deceased parents are present, seated around the group circle. Beside mourning and veneration, there is the fear of invading the space of the other. The work of re-finding one's lost parts must proceed cautiously, so as not to violate the space and identity of the other that is now so very precious" (H. Shmuel Erlich).

***

"Why is it impossible for an Israeli to tolerate the report of a German on his father? Because it arises positive feelings for this Nazi father to an unbearable extend in the Israeli who then threatened to leave this conference if the German would not stop. The staff member leader of this Small Study-Group prolonged-transgressed the session by 30 minutes!

Only one group member noticed it but didn't say a word until the day after, and that in form of a reproach ...

An Israeli member said to his German colleague that the German wanted the Israeli's aggressive reaction, that he provoked it. The German unaware of this, felt guilty towards the Israeli though he 'only' reported his difficult feelings of loving his perpetrator father, but it dawned on him that the Israeli was right and that he himself did this for his moral relief as a dirty trick, unbelievable, but true. On the other hand the Israeli panicked, too, when he looked on what he did and that he 'had no choice' in doing otherwise.

These strong paradoxical death-wishes-reactions, often suppressed, in part pre-consciously intended happen at special junctions: when I need to take away the other's moral basis for my own survival. The moral destruction in this homosexual rape, this Nazism, anti-Semitism area of my personality deriving from unresolved catastrophe-existence anxieties is the process: to blame the other for one's own failure. Project it on him, identify it with him and finally kill him for it! The Israeli and the German carried the process with the help of the group and the staff member. They could become aware of it and feel in consequence mutually sorry while able to continue their way, each his, without a catastrophe falling from the sky, but within a new situation arising turning the pending catastrophe into a good situation of mutual trust and respect – both still trembling filling a glass of orange juice for the other.

It is built in, in the development of such an over cross action that a new good real situation suddenly sets in. In a way it is a wonder. What enabled the

Israeli to live through his suffering may have been that the German told him that following Nazareth I he asked his father (against severe resistances on both sides) what he really did during the Nazi period. A short while later this father died of an exacerbation of a psychosomatic disease" (Thomas Erdmann).

***

"A dream (after the first day): 'The heating system in our house has not only broken down but has also been removed. Without telling me, my wife has seized the initiative and done this without consulting me. I am horrified and strike out at objects around me in rage. A heating repairman shows up to repair the damage. The situation normalizes. Looking back, still in the dream, I make too much of the spitefulness of my wife as well as of the terrible results of my rage and the bottomlessness of my shame.

The return to which Hillel Klein was referring is 'Tschuwa' in Hebrew; is such a return to humanity possible? Or is it only an infantile wish, as in my manifest dream? The theme of my dream was destruction and repair of a heating system. 'Why all the excitement?' says my emotional amnesia in self-justification; 'after all, human warmth, i.e. humanity, is a just question of the right technique – keep cool!' Or is Tschuwa possible only over generations, in the historical dialectic of ongoing time and the transgenerational shaping of culture?

My wife's father was an SS guard in a concentration camp – and my wife?

My childhood home, with its actively Roman Catholic atmosphere, was factually if not in name among those who 'go along with the crowd';

And I? My repeated dreams about the *catastrophic loss of a carrying case*, dreams which in spite of many attempts at interpretation obstinately reprimand me: why? If only the worst thing in my childhood were the loss of a satchel (case)! But people disappeared out of my life, to my way of thinking without a farewell, wordlessly, enigmatically, leaving me shaken to the present day.

Thus I hope that one day Germans, including myself, and Israelis (again) will be able with one another to endure and make fruitful an ambivalence which is broad enough to include quarrels. As one Israeli expounded to me in a confidential discussion, that would be a sign of normality.

In Nazareth too, then, amnesia was at work: individually, collectively, transgenerationally. Much remained unsaid. Are most things unsayable?

What do 'most things' mean? Have we Germans finally done enough to spell out, interpret, experience and materialize the words 'humanity' and 'atrocity processing' (A. Mitscherlich)? No, 'the past in the present', in this respect, is all the more a factor, when there is no differentiation between fantasy and reality, with a consequent inability to counteract the inroads of National-Socialistic transgenerational fantasies in our daily actions. I often toss and turn with nightmares at home; but here I slept after two nights as if in Abraham's bosom. Some of my patients prefer a life without dreams and/or therapy rather than to experience 'the past in the present'. The father of one female patient of mine was overseer of a Nazi company of convicts. She purportedly never dreams. The father of another patient was member of a firing squad. The patient broke off therapy in fury before clarification was possible.

Another dream (next-to-last day): 'Sad to say, I must live for a long time in a psychiatric clinic. The Chairperson of the German Psychoanalytic Association is of no avail here. As if that was not strange enough, and contrary to expectations, I don't feel abandoned by God and the world in this hopeless situation. Again and again, I woke up during this night with an ongoing inner peace, and I woke up again and again just to reassure myself of this unfailing inner quietude.'

The conference hotel, it appears, is unobtrusively guarded night and day. Briefly I experienced fear for myself, for the Israelis, for the Palestinians. It is strange: Israelis watch over me, child of one of Hitler's bystanders. My fantasy of the vengefulness of the Jews emerges clearly into consciousness against this background. My physical aches and pains are almost all gone. Rachel: I sat, unbearably forlorn, for the first time next to this Jewish woman colleague who grew up in pre-Nazi Germany; she turned the conversation during the evening meal to her sorrow over the loss of the German-Jewish culture. She now works in a 'Center for Remembering the Holocaust', where she helps older persons who were persecuted during the Holocaust to sort their recollections out of the amnesia which has dominated in the past and to narrate them on videotape as a memento to the families of their children and children's children" (Christoph Biermann).

***

'Milked' with Poison

"Looking for the roots of conflicting experiences, a Second Generation Jewish woman staff-member from Israel spoke about an idea with words and pictures. In a plenary she said, 'I was "milked" with tears.' This remark made a German non-Jewish member completely restless. The German woman had to look for an answer, although she could not know what she was looking for and whether or not it could be something to share with the others.

That evening she was in a self-analytic process and she found what she was looking for. She was very frightened about it and felt very alone with what she had found.

Next morning in the Small Study Group she could no longer bear to be alone with the unbearable and she gave a sign, which the consultant and the group picked up. They wanted to understand her. Both the group and the consultant helped her. The consultant found words for her feeling of something unbearable in the room and then, especially from a Jewish Israeli member came in her support in asking the German woman to share what was so unbearable for her. She could not believe this and so questioned the Israeli: 'Do you want to share *poison*?' Everyone responded with a courageous 'yes' giving her courage and so she told her story. She told about her experience of coming to the conference with the conviction that *all Jews would be same*. But then, she came to realize that Jews as individuals are as different as one would find individuals in any other group of people. Then she questioned herself as to why she needed so much work to find out what she had always known, that people are different. Step by step she 'deconstructed' the idea that all Jews are the same 'as a symbol of the fantasy of killing them'.

Now she had found the answer she had been looking for. For the first time in her life, she dared to share this truth about herself with others. The answer was, '*I was "milked" with the poison of the Nazi-idea*'. Her self-revelation had brought tears the evening before and now tears were flowing again as she met with the others while talking about her self-revelation.

There have been others besides these two who have been able to trace their unconscious fantasies of being 'milked' with tears or poison. Mainly women, who were born shortly after the war had, and independent from each other, came to similar discoveries and similar pictures. At the time, not all realized that 'to be milked' is not the same word or meaning for being nursed. In that moment, it seemed like this error was not important and it seemed like everyone understood what was being talked about. In his report, Shmuel Erlich (2000) gave a hypothesis about this error; that of its being a sign pointing to the unconscious experience of being nursed in the same moment as being milked, and with this, being emptied. It is as if the mothers needed to bear their children shortly after the war 'as a source of liveliness, hope and confirmation of the possibility of a future'. I am not yet convinced that the sons that were born during these years were nursed differently in a systematic way, although during the conference, even though they were much less in number, one of the German sons rattled off that he always received 'fresh potatoes' to eat from his mother. The manner in which he spoke about this seem to imply that he got bored with eating the fresh potatoes even though it seemed to be a special treat given to him by his mother. We need time to understand more about this and maybe we will come to the realization that also with this point there is more than one truth. To accept this may be difficult, especially for those coming from the Christian tradition" (Eva Maria Staudinger).

***

"It was April 1999, one of those dark days of Europe, Miloševitz. I am In Leicester Conference. University campus, Tavistock, group relations, Bion after WWII. I am a member of a small study group whose consultant is a young afro-American woman, British and Danish men in the group are talking about their sexual fantasies of Jewish women. A very distinguished British clinician is telling me about his group in the institutional event which deals with 'the Jewish stuff', showing the familiar hand gesture to indicate money, later I reveal that they deal with the issue of 'Accountability and the work of the unconscious'.

I am confused and scared not knowing how to absorb this new data to my experience there and to my Jewish identity as a whole. I am surprised to find comfort by talking, the first time in my life, to a German member in the conference who turned to be a real 'mensh' and becomes a friend.

From there, the way to Bad Segeberg is short, not without ambivalence enacted by missing the connection flight from Italy to Germany.

It was summer 1969, Roger's Plan is in the air. Goldman, the President of the Zionist Movement is talking to Nasser, the Egyptian President. I'm in

France, student conference, massive attack from all European community, but an Italian, again, like the German guy in 1999. A Turkish student is accusing me of being a racist when I explain the superiority [than] of the Israeli soldiers over the Arab soldiers. Attack on linking, Bion, me, a racist?

Summer 2000, Bad Segeberg, plenary session, a beautiful German woman (Stereotype of the female SS in movies?) says: *'I have an ordinary Nazi mother'*. The lake and the forest are so beautiful, the 'Apple-Kuchen', the Herring and the 'Kartofhel-Salad' are so tasty. I am in a small study group with German consultant, always critical towards him, difficulty to accept German authority, and here it comes, *'I have the ordinary Nazi-Jewish mother'*, me? Again attack on linking.

How could I say such an awful thing about my mother? Why of all places, I found it in Germany? Cruelty and beauty dwell together? Intelligence and prejudice dwell together?

April 2001, the dream of peace in the Middle East is evaporating, Leicester Conference, a very delicate negotiation with management to help/allow celebrating Passover Seder. Four Israelis and all together less than ten Jews are sitting around a very large table with many non-Jewish guests. I'm proud of the possibility to tell the 'whole world' the story of 'let my people go' (don't forget the 'other' people), not feeling at ease with the saying in the 'Hagada' *'Pour out Thy wrath upon the nation that know Thee not.'* Through the end of the Seder, a lovely old melody of traditional song from my father's home is coming from a German-Jewish psychoanalyst who couldn't participate in Bad Segeberg, exclusion again.

May 2001, last scene. I'm helping my mother to re-arrange her house towards her old age, a picture of a beautiful woman is getting out of an envelop, *'this woman was a friend of your father in the hospital in Germany'*, my mother tells me, at last, helping me to include.

There is never a 'last scene' in this endless story. Summer 2001, the German Foreign Minister Fischer is visiting the Middle East asking Arafat, after a horrible attack on a youth club in Tel-Aviv, whether he can uproot terrorist activity, Arafat asked back whether he, Fischer can uproot anti-Semitism" (Daniela Cohen).

***

Remembered Moments: Narratives of Critical Events

For each participant there are moments in a conference that are remembered long after, even years after the conference is over. The 'remembered moments' are not only remembered, they become objects of continuous work, they are viewed and reviewed, worked through in an attempt to make sense and gain understanding. These may be very personal moments, not necessarily witnessed or shared by others, or they can be moments that happened in the open, shared or witnessed by others.

Of special interest are those moments which are remembered by several participants, yet are seen from different perspectives, at times complementary and at others contradictory. In what follows there are examples of this: the same event, the different experiences.

The 'System Event' has a special place in the 'remembered moments'. This is not surprising since this event provides the stage for the unconscious dramatic enactment of the central issues of the conference.

The System Event is different from other events in the conference. It is the event in which the participants divide themselves into groups (all the other grouping are predetermined by the staff – be it the Plenary in which all participants take part, the Small Study Groups composed of mixed nationalities, or the Review and Application Groups composed of the same nationality). There is a good deal of physical movement in the System Event: participants move between groups, between different spaces and localities. The Management is available to interact and be observed by participants, so there is also movement to and from the Management room. A currency of "Working Hypotheses" about what is going on is established. All of this creates a lively setting, which at moments can become chaotic, and carries the danger of disintegration. The investment in this event and reflections on it occupy a central position in the 'remembered moments' of the conference.

The 'System Event' commences on the second day of the Conference. It acts as a new beginning: some of the preliminary anxiety wore off, a fledgling orientation to the space, the way of working and the different people begins to develop. The event starts in simultaneous but separate plenaries for the Israelis and the Germans, and lasts for 7 sessions. This is the first time these two nationality groups meet as two groups in the conference, and it is also their opportunity to get a feel of the "same nationality" as it is experienced in the here and now. Being together at this point in time arouses familiar as well as unexpected feelings. Following the initial sub-group plenaries there is a possibility for the groups to divide in order to form new groups that will pursue the Primary Task of the System Event. Along what lines will the participants divide themselves? Who will the leaders be? In what form will leadership be exercised? What will be the themes for discussion on the overt level? What will they be on the covert level? Each of the subgroups has its own development, issues, culture and ways of interaction. During the entire event the staff works in public, formulating understandings as to what is going on in the system as a whole on the basis of such information as it may have, and communicating these as working hypotheses. No wonder that so many contributions from participants have to do with this event.

Nazareth I

The first Nazareth conference was a journey in an uncharted land: 'Like traveling where no one has been before us.'
  It started in a plenary, with 55 participants – staff and members. It was a large room, the staff sitting at the one end of the room in a long line with Eric Miller as director in the middle, and Kathy White, the American Associate Director to his side. The 46 members sat in four prearranged rows of chairs. The first exchange was already mentioned: 'I am disappointed', says a German participant, 'why are there so few Israelis?' 'If you had not killed so many of us there would be more,' was the immediate answer. The level of anxiety, high to begin with, rose as this interchange took place. It did not take long before the unease with the seating arrangement was mentioned by someone: 'I am not comfortable sitting here, I can't see everybody, only the backs of people.' Another one joined the complaint, and someone said: 'Let's rearrange the chairs!' Within a few moments chairs were moved and rearranged so that now there was a huge circle along the walls of the large room. Some of the chairs were in front of the others disturbing the 'view'. The staff that did not move their chairs was engulfed by the big circle. In this havoc there were two participants, sitting one near the other, a German woman and a German man, who did not move their chairs. They became an island that was symbolically holding the center. Now members could more or less see each other, but had to shout to be

heard. It was again 'not comfortable'. Someone said: 'I did not want to move but the majority decided, so I went along'.

Did the majority decide? Was it checked? Within 10 minutes into the conference there was a call for action and the 'mob' streamed on in disregard of the prearranged structure or individual desire. This was the first appearance of the 'Past in the Present'. The two members who did not go along with the crowd were veterans of a previous Group Relations Conference – they were equipped with 'group pressure repellent'. This for me is a cherished moment. But – not for all.

***

"When we first all met in the large oblong (or was it square?) room, the seating arrangement was such that the leaders sat in a diagonal line, which separated in the manner of a roman phalanx, the leaders from the participants. The participants sat in a crowded half moon, the effect of which was that while the leaders could be seen by all, those members of the audience who dared to speak up could not be seen by the other who were listening, unless each one of them twisted his neck in ostrich-like fashion in order to do so.

You may remember that this setting alone aroused from the start rebellion against the management. When a sitting in the round was proposed one could feel great reluctance among the leadership to follow this proposal and in addition there was the odd opposition of two of the participants who refused to move into the circle. There was no explanation of their behavior; I obtained one only in private conversation with the lady who refused to move. She told me that she was so near sighted that she feared that she would not be able to recognize the face of whoever would be across from her. What motivated the leadership to be opposed to seating in round is unknown to me. Should I think that there was an initial plan to draw off the presupposed mutual antagonism in the group onto themselves? Did they wish to displace upon themselves the assumed unconscious antagonism between Germans and Israelis in order to facilitate the beginning of the discussion?" (Martin Wangh)

***

The first stage of the System Event

"We of the Israeli group debated among ourselves as to which topic to propose for joint work with our German colleagues. Several topics were raised, and I suggested the simple question: 'How is the past manifested in the present?' During the discussion a representative of the German group (Veronika) came over and proposed a topic that some of the Germans were interested in: 'The stereotypes that each nation has about the other'. Gila noted that this topic was similar to the one I had suggested. It did indeed seem that this was the case, and so Gila, Irena and I immediately – and, as it turned out, too hastily – left the Israeli group and joined a group of about twelve Germans. Within a few minutes another four Israelis joined us. With the assistance of the counselors we set up a work plan for that day.

It was agreed that at the end of the day we would decide (each group separately) what would take place at the two sessions that remained for the next day. I now recall this joint work as pleasant and 'business like' and most particularly as intriguing.

At the end of the day we separated – the Germans and the Israelis – so that each group could decide for itself how to continue Since all of us Israelis had the impression that productive work had been done, we should continue in the present format the following day as well.

At this point we were in for a great surprise. The Germans decided that they wanted to work with us for one session the following day, while keeping the last session as a 'purely German' forum, to clarify matters among themselves.

From this stage on my impressions become less and less objective.

Even the preceding impressions are not free from subjectivity, but in their case it seems to me that there should not be many differences of opinion about the facts. From this point on the impressions are also the facts, and so the picture I will draw is partial and perhaps egocentric, and anyone who wants to get a complete picture of what happened there should certainly not make do with the following description.

What the Israelis think

In the 'book of politeness rules' we subscribe to, there is a chapter on the ways of behaving in situations where one person is hurt by another. We acted according to these rules with respect to our German colleagues. We said that our opinion about our common future was different, but of course we respect their opinion, therefore we would work the next day according to their decision. The 'rules of politeness' helped us deal with the sense of insult we felt at first.

We Israelis then gathered to discuss what had happened. When we started talking to one another we immediately understood that it was a sample of 'the past in the present'. *The Germans had decided to remain together without the Jews.* The various reactions ranged from the desire to get up and leave the German group altogether to the idea of 'joining battle' – that is, broaching the topic the next day, since it was what we had come to the workshop for.

The force of exclusion was embarrassing. It was as if we were really 'over there' in the thirties and they were throwing us out. This led to equally forceful feelings of rage and the desire not to allow it to pass in silence. 'We'll show them this time' was the essence of our promise to ourselves 'to give them a good fight'.

That evening in our informal encounters with the Germans, I sensed the thin line between civilized European manners and the intense desire to tell them to go to Hell – between the human encounter with brave colleagues who had come to investigate a complicated issue together with us and the crazy feeling that the German bastards are once again establishing racial laws and organizing a 'purely German' forum for themselves.

The next morning

For me this session was the most important one in the whole Conference. It isn't fair to be selective, but I think about that session in particular again and again out of curiosity to see those moments, which are so hard to reconstruct, when that something occurred to make the whole thing an emotionally real event.

We really did 'give them the good fight'! We told the Germans that, even though there are accepted rules according to which they had decided what to do, and we respect their decision, something else had nevertheless taken place here on the level that is generally not talked about – but here in this conference it was absolutely essential and must therefore be explicitly discussed. On this level, the Germans had once again remained together by removing the Jews from among themselves. We said that the difference between then and now is that these Jews have somewhere to go, and that now they can tell the Germans to go to Hell.

This time the shock was theirs. At first they didn't understand. Then they tried to explain, and, worst of all, to apologize if they had hurt us. Their explanation was that after all *they had acted according to the rules*, they hadn't done anything illegitimate, and this was the majority decision, and so on and on. It took time till they too heard the chilling tones that we had heard the night before. For them too the 'yesterday' appeared in the 'today'.

I thought about the nightmare of those who had confronted the Germans back then, without a state or a guesthouse in Nazareth. I had some thoughts about my mother and the indescribable fear she had experienced towards the Germans, and about what it means that I am here. She will never forgive them, and perhaps it would be better to remain far from all this and leave the attempts to get closer to later generations.

Another line of thought also developed out of these free-floating associations. I imagined them to myself – faces most of which I did not know well. When they told us that this was a majority decision (for the Germans to remain by themselves) I tried to guess who had voted 'against us' – who had such a Nazi face. I made a selection, I divided them into good ones and bad ones, and I 'knew' that I could tell the difference. Later I thought that *'they are all the same'* and that all of them should be finally eliminated. They deserve it – after all, they're Germans. I even thought about how to do it.

When they gradually began to understand what had happened when they had decided to have a 'German-only' session, I was left empty and wanted to get away from these people who had evoked this sort of hatred in me. I remember the next session vaguely; I wasn't really listening. I have no idea what led me, at some point, to listen for their names and to connect their names with their faces. First it happened and only afterwards did I notice that it was happening. I played with the names, some of them foreign and cold – Rolf, Gertrude, Carl, Werner, Ziegfried, Thomas – and some softer – Michael, Gisela, Veronika, Christoph, Uschi. I know it won't seem strange if I say that gradually, to my total surprise, they began to seem human" (Yoram Hazan).

***

A German perspective

"The first session of the System Event took place in the late afternoon of the second day.

The Germans' meeting was later described by some of the participants as *'tumultuous and chaotic'*. One reason for this was surely that it was the first time all of the German participants were sitting together in a group. Already stressed to nerve's end by their trip and arrival on the previous day, the still existing unfamiliarity, the beginning of the conference and the previous small group sessions and plenary, they now found themselves confronted by a large group situation which was not pre-formed and, in other words, had no securing structures. They were faced with the task of making decisions during this 90-minute session about the goals they wanted to pursue and where they wanted to meet from that point on. Under such circumstances, tumult and chaos are never far away.

One basic tendency, which I initially represented most clearly, was aimed at forming a subgroup which would offer the Israeli colleagues joint sessions. Others were in favor of this idea and towards the end of the session one participant jumped up and suggested that whoever was interested in proposing to the Israelis that we talk about the stereotypes we have of each other should join her. Anyone who has had experience with group dynamics knows the kind of drama that unfolds at such a moment, which looks like a storm in a teacup from the outside.

Soon 11 interested participants had got together, and the group that was formed in this way immediately made the woman who had taken the initiative its emissary in order to bring this proposal to the Israelis who were meeting in a different room.

During this first session of the system event, the Israelis, for their part, had also discussed the idea of working together with the Germans, but with a much calmer, wait-and-see attitude. As it turned out, seven members of the Israeli group followed the German suggestion.

In the second session of the system event, on the evening of the second day, in the first session of the group of Israelis and Germans that had just been formed, both sides agreed to meet together at first and then, after this session was over, to split up into their separate national subgroups to think about how the five remaining sessions of the system event should be organized on the following day and the day thereafter.

The group's decision was to propose meeting together with the Israelis in four sessions and to hold the last session with the other Germans, but without the Israelis. Driven by the nagging feeling of having done the wrong thing, I could not let the leader of the majority opinion announce the group's decision on his own, but had to go with him in order to voice my dissenting opinion.

The Israelis had decided to propose to the Germans that they stay together until the end of the system event. So, when the groups advised each other of their respective results, the Israelis seemed surprised and hurt. My heart stopped. My attempts to mitigate the German position went unheard. After all, I had gone along with it. The Israelis accepted the German proposal.

Consciously and in the present, the Germans had had good reasons for their decision. There was a definite wish to think about the only session in which the German group had met as a whole. I had a different view of the matter. I can talk to Germans when I'm in Germany, I thought; here the partners in dialogue are the Israelis. To meet without them would mean excluding them. Although it was only a matter of one out of five sessions, everything shifted to this one session in a symbolic condensation. 'The Germans are excluding the Jews', is what kept pounding in my head. Although I had voted against the majority opinion, I had not taken a stand against the result. I should have said: 'I'm not going along with this!'

At first I was totally absorbed by the attempt to find out how I could have behaved differently, I instead slowly began looking at how I had actually behaved. I had gone against my clear intention and yielded to the majority option. I remembered Hillel Klein's statement: *'The bystanders are the problem'*.

When the session began, Israelis and Germans were sitting at a considerable distance from each other in two straight rows of chairs. I noticed that, without realizing it, I myself had sat down right in the middle of the Germans and was sitting directly across from a slender, blond man sitting right in the middle of the Israelis. He's the one with whom I will have to bring about the necessary clarification, I thought. Only later did I note his name. It was Yoram.

The Israelis seemed convinced that the Germans were not even aware of what they were doing. The Germans got a strong dose of this during the third group session of the system event. The Israelis' main reproach stemmed from the conviction that the Germans had no idea what it meant to set up a 'pure German group'. The Israelis called it a 'cold-hearted decision'.

The seating arrangement I described before cast Yoram and me in leadership roles. Yoram made himself the spokesman for the Israeli group. He hammered his anger into the Germans sitting across from him. I only picked up fragments of what Yoram had to say. My attention during this session was paralyzed by an illusionary failure to recognize something, which may have been caused by the recurrence of something that had been repressed, surely through the stimulation of frequently seen images charged with powerful emotions: *The Jews sitting across from me looked like a conspiratorial unit without individual features.* The dehumanizing process of the past had caught up with the participants of the group conference here. This was true of both sides, as I realized later. Just as I lost my eye for the individuality of the Israelis sitting across from me, their blindness to the present made faceless Nazis of the 11 easily distinguishable men and women from Germany who were sitting across from them.

The heated exchange of words gradually cooled down, and this continued into the next session. I was upset by the intensity of the profound hatred, got very caught up in thought, hardly listened any longer, but, as the group atmosphere slowly settled down, noticed how the seven Jews sitting across from the Germans began to look more like individuals, had names which I tried to remember if I did not know them yet. More differentiated feelings of like and dislike began to fill the images at hand with life. In retrospect, this process of re-individualization was for me the most impressive moment of the first conference to separate the past from the present.

The Germans reversed their decision. The whole group stayed together until the last session of the system event" (Carl Nedelmann).

***

Another Version of the same event

"During the whole conference, but especially during the System Event, I began to feel that, as a German, I belong to the embodiment of evil and inhumanity. There were small events, almost to-be- neglected remarks by one or the other of the Israelis, accumulating to this feeling which I would not have been able to put into words, then. Being perceived in this way was nothing new in my personal history but never before had it been so totally impossible to escape this perception.

And: never before did I have to experience the true aspects of it. Yet, I believe that there was a strong unconscious wish to escape this truth, and in my view the early split-up of the German group had been a symptom of defence against it.

However, working with our Israeli colleagues led into the very experience I/we had hoped to escape from.

Both Germans and Israelis had tried to share during the System Event some of the 'secrets we have before each other'. This was scaring for all of us, and we could not begin before the consultants we had asked for arrived. Then, one of the Israelis suspected that, if they were in Germany today, they might be persecuted like their parents. I answered that this was the very thought I had also had the day before: Even today the Israelis might not be safe with us; and moreover, *I did not feel safe with them. If they were less civilised they would not let us go home again, but kill us in revenge.*

Obviously, it was not enough to have these thoughts and anxieties spelt out – we had to enact them:

There were two more sessions within the event and both subgroups had to decide how to continue for these sessions. Within the German subgroup, there was a clear vote for continuing with our Israeli colleagues. Then, the idea came up to investigate again in what happened in the German group in the first session of the system event. Didn't the speed in which we separated from the rest of the Germans indicate that there was something about being German which we did not want to face? Could we find out together with the other Germans what we had tried to avoid? These thoughts puzzled us so that we suggested to the Israeli colleagues to continue together for one more session and then meet with the other Germans for the last session. From the Israelis, we received the suggestion to continue together for both remaining sessions.

When we met again for the session which we had agreed upon, our Israeli colleagues confronted us with what our suggestion had meant to them: We had decided once again – like our parents' generation – to free ourselves from Jews, to have another 'Großdeutschland' without them.

We were thunder-struck! We began to argue, to explain, to elaborate, even to excuse ourselves, we fought for almost the whole session — but we were not able to change the picture we had produced.

For me, two remarks from the Israelis helped me to gradually grasp some of what had happened:
1. Even if we had not intended to throw them out, this was in fact what we had done; and even if we did not mean to get rid of them, this was what it meant to them.
2. We gave the impression that we did not want to do our dirty washing in front of them.

These two remarks were the ones which 'reached' me. Finally we, the German subgroup, revised our decision and agreed to continue with our Israeli colleagues also for our last session, if they were still willing to continue with us – which they were.

Through correspondence with one of the Israeli members after the conference I came to understand more of what had happened to myself in this situation. I think that the issue of shame had indeed been basic for me. I had understood that the early split-up of the German group during the system event had been an attempt to avoid facing my own destructiveness. Therefore, I wanted to try and face it by facing the 'other Germans' which I had left behind. However, if I could hardly bear this confrontation myself, how could I bear the Israelis witnessing it? The attempt to avoid being identified by our Israeli colleagues, as the destructive fascist aggressor, made me become this aggressor for them.

And yet, there also was a sign of hope: The Israelis had confronted us, and we, the Germans, had changed our minds" (Veronika Grueneisen).

***

And another one: Tumult and the "Führer Principle"

"In the 'pure German' group at the beginning of the System Event, I was as if paralyzed by a compulsion to go along with the crowd. After half-heartedly advancing a discussion motion in support of a possible subgroup on

'Germans and Jews in the German Psychoanalytic Association', I withdrew into silence. The group situation was dominated by 'Fight and Flight' (Bion, 1960); my thought of suggesting to seek a discussion structure by forming a panel of moderators became inwardly entangled in the fantasy that this would meet with incomprehension, indifference and scorn. I found no further ideas; it was as if my mind were void. No: I did not belong to the 'Resistance', and there was no resistance to be found in the group of the Germans at this moment. John Rittmeister or Helmuth James von Moltke were not our models and teachers. As we wrestled with our divisions, three female members dominated the group's marked need to subordinate itself. We 'pure' Germans succumbed to the 'Führer Principle'.

In 'my' German subgroup, we decided – I would say 'head over heels' – to discuss mutual prejudices of Jews and Germans; we succeeded in inviting Israeli participants, who were initially impressed by the difference between German 'effectiveness' and their own entrapment in discussion. In addition, the majority of the Germans officially voted to subsequently hold a pure German session without the Israelis. This met with determined resistance from the Israelis who had joined the group. In a passionate debate, the Israelis advanced the interpretation that the Germans were in the process of eliminating the Jews. They would not put up with it!

At this point I can quote from Yoram Hazan's 'Nazareth Impressions' (with his permission). Yoram, one of the Israeli participants in this group, describes the situation in retrospect as follows:

'We really did "give them the good fight" ... On this level, the Germans had once again remained together by removing the Jews from among themselves ...'

Survival: An (Un-)Canny Triumph of the Perpetrators?
In retrospect, I ask myself: What possible group and subjective dynamics did we German participants avoid at the beginning of the System Event with our orientation to basic assumptions like 'Fight-Flight' and 'Dependency'? My experience of the previous, mixed Small Study Group left me with the embarrassing memory of how German participants among themselves compulsively walled off passionate feelings, particularly hatred, and brought outbursts under control, and how the persons who were controlled submitted to this control as accomplices, without asserting the right to resist.

Based on this previous experience, I think as a psychoanalyst of the following hypothesis: The group of pure German participants unconsciously began by repeating the dehumanizing activity of the Nazis and directing it initially against themselves – in other words, a bit of the 'Past in the Present' ...

Yet another moment was reminiscent of the stifling of affects. At the beginning of the System-Event, the Germans and the Israelis met in two separate groups at the behest of the staff. This 'just-us-Germans-hour' renders me unexpectedly helpless and speechless: I seem to myself to recognize the same signs of collective hectic activity, arrogance, despair and foolishness as those found in reports of the Nazi era. Subsequently the affect-stifling defenses appeared to me to have gained the upper hand: we Germans took refuge by splitting head-over-heels into groups and falling into line behind three female leaders of three different sub-groups. Yes, 'refuge': refuge from the moment of latent truth, which might have surfaced in the experience of the group as a whole. And what truth would that have been?" (Christoph Biermann)

***

One of the dynamics of the System Event had to do with a group of three participants who located themselves geographically in the farthest area and became more and more withdrawn and disconnected from the rest of the event. This group consisted of a German-Jewish female and two men: an Israeli and a German. As the sessions went on it seemed to the staff that 'the unacceptable' was projected by the whole membership into this sub-group, creating a high-risk situation of madness. The 'unacceptable' was understood by the staff group to be the bringing together of the Jewish-ness and the German-ness as personified by the German-Jewish member. The larger group eliminated this unacceptable element by evacuating it into this sub-group. It took the staff several working hypotheses to give meaning to what went on and what was symbolized by the action until this conflict of joining the incompatible elements could be owned by the membership as a whole, which in turn freed this sub-group from that burden.

***

"One may ask oneself, why already just at the beginning of this experience the thought arose in the German group to make small groups and to distribute them among different rooms (territories); instead of this, why not use the opportunity, in at least one of the seven sessions, to start with a large group with clear processes, to take the time and to ask questions and to develop a starting concept. At some point during the course of this SE, vague suspicions arose that could have created fear in the German group that they were numerically superior to the Israeli group. The thought was lost, but once again surfaced later in a plenum and intensified itself into an image of 'Greater Germany' that was, after the war divided up into Western Germany, the German Democratic Republic and in Poland/Russia. And it was then recalled that the reuniting of the two parts (of Germany) after the political turning point in 1989, triggered off immense fears.

The smallest of the three German groups which formed themselves in the SE, disappeared during the progress of the System Event; the group lost territory and the eight participants lost themselves inside one of the other two German groups.

What has continually baffled me up till today is the fact that I found myself exactly in this small group that, with its later destiny, reflected an aspect of my life as one born in Eastern Prussia and who was driven into Western Germany.

Splitting up the large German group was done chaotically. First, some were still speaking about their expectations and the understanding of the 'Primary Task' of the SE, when suddenly the whole group dissolved when other participants became active, stood up, stood behind spokesmen and declared that they wanted to join their group. During the commencing tumult of this dispersal, different mottos for group themes were called out and in a flash chairs were pulled back, this one hesitated, another rushed about, and in the end three circles were formed. The consultants sat there, wanted to present a comment about the current events, but nobody was listening.

I once again found myself in the group that wanted to devote itself to the special question of one of the members; it dealt with a question of identity. One of the consultants sat down with us and said that this question that is pointed at one member could lead the entire group down a dead-end; he suggested instead that every group member could deal with the question why he or she exactly joined this group; that meant, then, dealing with one's own part of the group theme.

That this advice was ignored was astonishing, or perhaps not. It indicated even already at this point that the staff was little thought of.

Our small group just survived a joint session in which the discussion intensified, as predicted, led down into a dead-end and awoke quite strong, aggressive feelings in many participants, which were also expressed.

In the following session, the group member who had initiated this group was, without any previous announcement, gone; mixed in with the consternation of those remaining – because of this disappearance without any ado – was anger about this unreliability, pangs of conscience about one's own vehemence and flying accusations. Thus shattered, we left our territory, searching for … another seat, another group, the missing member; and we lost this search, which led us through broad expanses of the hotel, as well as one member after the other in the perfumed rows of petunias and radiant nasturtiums.

Perhaps in order get a new impulse on how we could retackle the task of the SE, we remaining three took an observatory break with the staff.

Later, we tried to hook up with a group of eight Israelis who were sitting in open shade, and who seemed to be so lively in their discussion and at the same time calm and collected, not so excited. To our question about us joining them, came: 'It's not possible at the moment.'

Another German group appeared to us, in their tension-filled concentration on a speaking leader, so cold to new members that we had no impulse to settle down there.

We then landed into a group made up of Germans and Israelis (about 15 to 5), and we stayed together for five sessions, until the end of the SE.

Three main points have remained in my memory from these SE sessions.

1. A lack of group boundaries led to great emotional, intellectual and social insecurity for individual group members.

What does this mean? Just as we three remaining were willing to be allowed into the group, later we continually experienced that new groups came, old members of our group suddenly disappeared, reappearing or not. There was a continual coming and going, without anyone mentioning it. Only from a hint by one of the consultants was the group very gradually aware of how problematic this apparent liberalism and openness was. It had something to do with the great nonchalance and the disinterest of the group itself, and indicated that the group had not developed any awareness of itself and individual members. According to the consultant, this lack of boundaries was a sign that the group did not wish to work.

'Boundaries' are part of the concept of the Tavistock Conference and are not, like I thought at the beginning, rigid border lines, but should be more understood as border areas with a certain expanse, within which all possible social acts may occur: questions and answers, negotiations, discussions, various measures of closeness and distance, having to wait, being able to wait, in any case everything except 'taking somebody by surprise'. So, for example, in our group there should have been a 'door representative' to speak with each newcomer about their desires and who would have reported to the group, where it could have been discussed and decided. It should have been taken for granted that the group had an image of itself and its current interests. An Israeli group member, still in the phase of gradually understanding the facts, brought up the following point: *the group may behave thus and experience itself perhaps in such a way as well, as if it had no history, no continuality, no past and no responsibility.*

2. Even analysts 'with great occupational sensitivity and experience of emotions and subconscious processes' (Beland) got caught in the wake of the disorienting group processes.

In the ongoing course of the group sessions, much was said but there was such little content as to be worth thinking about. There was a horrible, intensifying atmosphere, and it was microscopically observable how statements and comments were taken as accusations and how assumed accusations were shifted on to others. It was an exceedingly difficult atmosphere, troubled, edgy, confused, injurious, helpless, but strong emotions remained locked up. A message from the management came to us which was supposed to have reflected our current state of consciousness and experience. Naturally, some asked themselves why the staff member had come exactly to this interpretation since he had no longer been at some sessions or had participated in group happenings in the SE – neither on the entire staff nor as an individual consultant. Anyway, the message concerned the point that the group could not tolerate that both (German and Jewish) were together. Because of this, members who were both (quite a few participants were Jewish and German), would be thrown out of the group – eliminated.

Indeed, during the group processes, the term 'eliminate' occurred a few times in the messages of the staff members, as well as other emotive words such as 'extinguish' and 'select.' It appeared to me that most in the group did not especially notice this, because there was no outcry, no visible symptoms of this; that this or any other term was heard which directly referred to the Nazi time.

Today, I ask myself when that which I learned in Nazareth passes before my eyes, why didn't I cry out instead of only communicating with my neighbor sitting next to me.

The staff remained on plan with their messages during the following sessions – to make a theme of the ambivalent relationship of the group participants concerning the 'German-Jews' (namely hate and attraction). A part of this 'German-Jew' could have been combined in one person or a couple. The statement was for me directed at showing that the group was in conflict, either working on the hate-filled projections on others or not; and simply expelling the hate. A German-Jewish couple could have been a model, how one may argue and yet remain together. One thinks here of Bion's most mature fundamental belief of a group, couple formation, in which a couple is ambivalently evaluated and desired because it is creative and it can create something new; this means, after a creative act – and this may be a argument that does not end in destruction – the couple brings about a mature solution.

I had the impression that the staff messages had triggered latently existent – but without critical reflection – spoken knowledge. Without targets and in the helplessness, the continued conversations were always horribly apparent and there were quite a few signs that the participants picked out others who could perhaps be used as scapegoats and could be made into Nazis.

I would like, however, to make clear how this inner process extended over many sessions.

The staff message about 'eliminating' spontaneously caused me intense stomach pain, which kept up for several days. Along with my involvement in the different group sessions, I attempted to comprehend which inner emotions were producing these symptoms in me. A dream in which I only saw the toilet in my bathroom as I was looking into the mirror and an incredibly strong attack on the staff, with a powerfully beating heart and feelings of fury during one of the last plenary sessions, made me aware that I projected negative feelings and prejudices despite my alert consciousness and I undertook many efforts to deposit inside the ugly – because hated – counterpart, these feelings as perceived by me, as the true qualities of the 'other'. As my inner state of mind became clearer to me, my stomach pain lessened and I could process that which caused the fury inside me. I understood that I did not want to really admit that I was furious with a Jewish member of the group and then also could not directly express this, but left this to another; that I dumped my fury instead onto the staff and only by this fantasized attack, could I think about it" (Angelika Zitzelsberger-Schlez).

***

The System Event is the playground for the exploration of unexpected, unconscious, unthought-of and unspeakable themes, as shown in what follows.

***

"It happened in the third plenary session of the first Nazareth Conference. Long before the workshop started I had been worrying whether anything antisemitic might crop up inside me leaving me behind with an intense and threatening feeling of shame.

This point came as a German participant had asked for a discussion or rather an explanation of the fact that the German group had split up into three on the first afternoon. It came to my mind immediately that one woman of the migrant group had presented herself and her colleagues as 'displaced persons' and that even then when it happened I had thought: *'she was like a German refugee seeking a new home'*.

So this to me was Germany divided into three: FRG, GDR, and the lost territories east of the Oder-Neisse-line. The first surprise to me came from the German side including German members of the staff. It took some explaining such as mentioning Eastern Prussia and Silesia to make myself understood and to clear up the confusion over the Iron Curtain and the Oder-Neisse-line. Only then, in the second place, the full blame hit me for not having cared enough for the Israeli members of the plenary which was expressed in terms of my taking an interest in lost territories instead of lost people.

Sharing my idea with the large group had apparently aroused a lot of anxiety and possibly hostility. The simple reason for this could have been that I had presented myself as a nationalist German crying over the loss of the German eastern territories.

I am rather certain, though, that this is not my position. I remember clearly advocating the once-and-for-all recognition of the Oder-Neisse-line in political students' groups as early as 1960, the year when I first came to Israel, by the way. I prefer to link the situation described to that moment of fright and great embarrassment when on the first day of the conference one German participant naively asked the question why the ratio of Israeli and German participants in the workshop was so lopsided, and when the immediate reply was: 'Why are you surprised, you killed them all.'

For many years only Germans on the far right side of the political spectrum have shown an interest in the division of Germany into three even coining the slogan of 'Germany tripartite – never.' The vast majority of my fellow countrymen and -women unconsciously preferred the situation as it was: the existence of the two smaller Germanies made it much easier to forget about German grandeur and along with it, about German crimes.

I believe that the division of the German group into three at the beginning of the System Event was, among other things, a desperate attempt not to be big, dangerous, and possibly aggressive. The repeated call by Israeli participants for us Germans to finally show our aggression against the Jews made sense at last, not because we Germans were necessarily so full of hatred, but because we were afraid even of the slightest sign of aggression against Jews. How can we be sure that we can control such feelings with most of us being children of Nazi Germany?

It was bothersome for the Israelis; I take it, to witness this very special German struggle. I think it would help the relations between Germans and Israelis as well, though, if we Germans came to grips with our natural size without being scared or scaring.

As for my mixed feelings of shame, hurt, anger, and of being turned away, I was able to sort things out with one of our Israeli friends in the evening. It happened so that we both felt a need for that. What I learned then was that his father had indeed lived in Breslau beyond the Oder-Neisse-line and was still fond of German culture without ever wanting to set his foot on German soil again, however. So here was someone who had really suffered more losses than one can take: his people, his territory and his country. I had been unaware of the possibility that among the Israelis present there might be someone to whom the territories east of the Oder-Neisse-line had a very special meaning.

It may well be that I was lacking concern when I made my comment in the plenary. I was not complaining about the loss of territory as I hope to have made clear. I think my Israeli colleague is right in his plea for mourning over the lost people, the lost Jewish people, though" (Armin Pollmann).

***

Nazareth II

The System Event in each conference has the same structure and the same Primary Task, and yet evolves differently and unearths new unexpected issues. Although each conference has different participants, many of whom are new comers to the event, we had the impression that each System Event was built on the previous ones, was more daring and moved all of us forward.

System Event

"Having to cope with the mourning and helplessness over past events and struggles of some of the participants, initially, was a burden that I felt enormous. It was amazing for me that no dynamic hay was made out of the contrast between, for instance, one member's inability to articulate properly a frightening event as a little girl sitting in a 'bunker' by the end of the war afraid of Russian soldiers raping and the inability of her mother to manage the situation by functioning as a protective shield, and her actually felt fear of anything resembling a dependent relationship which obviously stemmed from associating dependence with helplessness. Her discourse, however, did not elicit but a polite interest not going further to peculiarities of the presented scenery and to her expressed emotions. After moments of some staggering and unevenness a powerful idea came up in the group kindling imagination and a lot of turmoil. We all were grasped tightly by the issue of revenge. Henceforth, this SE-group was called 'Revenge Group'. Belonging and sticking to that group from now on for me was hard going emotionally but it gave me a sense that it had been worthwhile participating in 'Nazareth II'.

Culling my memories of what happened next, I have to admit that a scar from past injury stemming from early times in my life which already had been touched on in the SSG, preoccupied me very much: a tendency to withdraw vindictively in moments of not feeling respected or acknowledged, and thereby being ashamed within a group. In these instances I am prone to act, and, indeed, acted as a person who wraps eager attention around himself like a cloak of safety. I am acquiring the attitude of an observing ethnologist in order to protect myself. I had, and still have to pay for this particular solution of a problem because trust in the co-members of my group diminishes. In this case, trust in the members of the SE-Group vanished, and I felt more and more isolated. Trust, at this very moment, seemed to me a dangerous luxury. This separated me from those who, for example, decided innocently and playfully to make choices about which staff member and why to ask for consultancy. I was not up for playing anymore.

When one of the Israeli members invoked the shadow of 'Amalek' as a prototypical story of revenge-taking it touched me very much, and served as an incentive to grapple along with my problem. The biblical accounts dealing with fighting and destroying ruthlessly aside I was reminded of A. Galante Garrone's 'Amalek, il dovere della memoria' which I had read shortly before leaving for Israel. It recalled the importance of spelling out, and of creating narratives of traumatic memories, and of sharing them with trustworthy people.

All of a sudden the question popped in my mind: would it be possible for me to be or to become a trustworthy listener to Johanna, Chaim, Ruth, Mishael, Silvia, and the rest? Or did I have to withdraw in order to protect myself thus escaping from experiences of loss, grief, and rage? What I had learned at that moment is that one of the most important things I can do when being wrongly attacked or rebuffed, is talk about this to people. When some of the Israelis started to talk about what happened to them or to their families (probably not for the first time), they created an atmosphere which soon started to have strong effects on the listener as well as on the narrator.

I do not really know whether I have accomplished my striving to be a trustworthy audience, when Israelis and Jews began to tell their stories of abuse, victimization, loss, and grief. Anyhow, trying to do so will remain an ongoing task lest the law of forgetting and denial, still very strong even in actual German society of which I form a part, might be perennial. This is what I found most rewarding.

Soon after my return to Germany I had the opportunity to read Myriam

Anissimov's recently published biography of Primo Levi. This book had a very great impact on me, partly because 'Nazareth II' was ever present in my mind's eye.

Was Hety Schmitt-Mass right when she wrote in a letter to Primo Levi: 'As to understanding the Germans, you will certainly never achieve that: even we ourselves will not arrive at doing that, because things have happened, at that epoch, which never should have occurred'?

I ask myself what would happen if some of these Germans are eager and able to listen to the individual stories from survivors of the Holocaust or from the second and third generation. Would that help the darkness of the Nazi-German period to be illuminated starkly and movingly, in a way that provides human teaching for others and, at the same time, human relationships as well?" (Odo Schulte-Herbrüggen)

***

"When, after one year, I am able to see what the second Nazareth Conference means to me, the incident which most stands out for me is my furious and confused attack on the staff during the last plenary session on the last day of the conference. *'I am seething':* I fired off, in German, these words at Eric Miller, the conference leader. I attacked the entire staff – and especially Eric Miller as the responsible one – because two staff members, at the least, had not satisfactorily fulfilled their duties.

From the previous Tavistock Conference in Israel, from the staff's description of their commitments in the Nazareth brochure, from a paper by Eric Miller, I know that the adherence to time, territory and tasks are among the central commitments of the staff at the Leicester Conference.

During the last plenum meeting, I attacked the staff member for the lax handling of his own rules and that he – and this is the point which I hold against him- nonchalantly disregarded what appeared to me as a lack of conscience. I attempted to clarify that my trust in the staff member's honesty was shaken by this. That I can no longer accept that he also means what he says and that because of this I felt myself quite abandoned. I also stand by my criticism still today, but it is important to say that the vehemence, with which I made Eric Miller start, has a background. Here I would like to emphasize that I am happy about my shaken trust in the staff and especially in my shaken trust in the idealized 'father figure', Eric Miller. Because of this, I have found the inner strength to rehabilitate my natural father.

In order to make what was said clear, reverting back to the past is necessary. I was at the 1988 conference in Jerusalem, with the theme 'The Meaning of the Holocaust for Those Who were not Directly Effected,' and I had spoken in my small group about an important discovery about my father, who at that point in time had already been dead 10 years. I do not want to completely repeat the story that I told at that time, rather only the point that was used by a Jewish group observer as excuse to express his hatred of the German Nazis by disparaging my father. In the group I explained that I had received – just before the conference – some of my father's personal papers from my mother, among other things, a thin writing pad containing notes from a medical lecture in Königsberg in 1938. At that time, my father had noted down the official school of thought, that with psychologically ill people, sterilization must be carried out because their illness was hereditary. And in the group, I concerned myself with the question what it could have perhaps meant to my father that his eldest son, my 20-year-old brother Alexander, had become ill with a schizophrenic-affective psychosis.

Today, I am proud of my past contribution and above all proud that I, unprotected, could express my doubt and insecurity because only through this can I feel my way to the 'truth'. About a half a year later, I received a copy of an interview from a German participant of this conference, which had been done in America by Mr. X, the then group observer. Mr. X was present at the meeting in which I had spoken and he had heard what I had said. In his interview, he spoke against a German participant who was suffering because her father had been an active Nazi who was engaged in euthanasia. Mr. X had lied. At that time, I was outraged and I wanted to write to him but the German participant advised me against this because it would not have had any purpose anyway. Over the past 9 years, I have always wondered why I did not write to Mr. X, in order to set his claims straight, 'even if it had no purpose', which means even if I could not have convinced him that his hatred and his search for revenge had distorted his perceptions. It seemed to me as if I had secretly agreed with Mr. X. I could not contradict this because, internally, I had depreciated my father. Searching for truth and truthfulness, I had oriented myself to other 'fathers' and this was indeed to *idealized Jewish fathers* whose utterances and behavior I never held in doubt until the second

Nazareth Conference. They always appeared more credible, and thus *I had betrayed my natural father.*

Something else which concerns this is also important. After the first conference in Nazareth in 1994, I had an impression of each of the 40 participants at that time. It could have been a conversation, a gesture, an expression, a deed. I could connect something personal with each of the forty names – but with one single individual not. If I read this name in the participant's list, he was a nobody to me. And this participant has the same first name as my father: Siegfried.

I believe that it is understandable why I am thankful that at Nazareth II I could finally call into question my idealizations, and get a more realistic view of credibility and implausibility. The groundwork for my outburst against the staff member had been prepared, among other things, in my System Event group.

It was this tiresome System Event that for my feelings and my experiences touched my emotions most deeply; above all suppressed, unpleasant emotions were stirred up. I do not know who suggested the title 'revenge'; perhaps it was Ruth who wanted to work on this. I thought about it, it made me afraid; I also did not really know if I really could start with something like this, and yet, with a vague feeling, I indeed decided for this group. I also searched for the place with the greatest fear because based on my experience from earlier Tavistock Conferences, this had mostly brought me the greatest profit.

We were two Germans, an Israeli man and two Israeli women.

Right at the beginning, I remembered that years ago at a congress in Germany a participant from this group had asked me the question, if I was afraid of revenge by Jews. At that time, I was for the very first time confronted with such a thought and I was then always preoccupied with this question. During my first Leicester Conference in Zichron Yaacov, Israel, in 1992, I was in a Jacuzzi one evening with some other Conference participants. On this second day, we were still strangers; I got into a conversation, in the steaming water, with a young woman and she said to me that she didn't have anything against the Germans, but was sensitive to hearing the German language. Three days later, very late at night, I was swimming in the hotel swimming pool; except for me there were three Israeli men who were also participants in the conference. The atmosphere became somewhat threatening because of the dim light, the steamed up glass panes and naturally, because of the churned up emotions of the just-experienced group session, and suddenly my heart started beating wildly and I got a horrible attack of fear. I was afraid that the three men, who were just then slowly swimming nearby me, could drown me.

About one year later, at a group congress in Heidelberg, it was clear to me in a seminar that I was very disappointed that some contacts with Israelis, which had been established with great friendliness and mutual empathy, could not be further developed over distances. 'This is perhaps revenge,' said an Israeli participant.

I brought my experiences along to the small group at Nazareth II. I no longer recall what the reaction was, and also no longer remember many other contributions. My German colleague in our group was asked during a session what she associated with the subject of revenge. She darkened greatly and sat there, retreating into herself. Then she spoke about feelings for revenge in connection with the relationship to her mother.

In a session, a short scrap occurred between me and the other German woman which I soon attempted to block off. I had the impression that I was becoming the victim of her mother projections and I felt no desire to clarify that with her. During another group session, I was suddenly extremely uneasy about our mutual different efforts to deal with this complicated theme professionally and with mutual understanding. I thought, and also said it aloud: 'It is too beautiful to be true!' that we are sitting here, the daughters and sons of victims and culprits and to have such a civilized, profound contact with one another. An Israeli woman, who at the beginning of the cooperative work spoke about her very conflicting feelings, felt a strong tension in our group and assumed that there were erotic fantasies.

From my notes, I infer that we were very frustrated as a group because our attempts at contact with the other sub-systems were first rejected by all. Nobody wanted to sit together with us and to do an exchange. We felt like the 'shit' of the entire conference and like we were handled as lepers. Was it our theme that had mobilized my deepest, archaic feelings for my experiences?

It was also thus in the working group. There were moments of trust and affection and great openness, contrasting with sudden expressions of mistrust and rejection, more pronounced and stronger then in the 'led' Small Study Group. With me, doubts then emerged whether the perceived friendly interaction was real and meant personally, or used as a means to an end, in order to 'tease out' as much as possible. Looking back, my impression becomes firm that we as a group spoke not only about revenge (impulses, fantasies, carry it out), but rather how the dynamics in this small group (which was the smallest in this event) got out of control from time to time. This was the burning reason from which I experienced and reflected on the 'failure' of two staff members, and what I in the end vented in the outbreak described above, because one mistrustful thought of becoming prey as a German took the upper hand.

I was seething. This is how I entitled my report. What has remained is an agreeable skepticism concerning 'adults' (an interpretation is hiding behind this!) and their 'promises'. In addition, what has remained is the certainty that I have the right to clearly and aggressively face Mr. X. This is what I learned at Nazareth II" (Angelika Zitzelsberger-Schlez).

***

"In the last plenary I dropped my pen and looked around whether anybody had noticed it. I was suddenly scared by a member's open conflict with a staff member over taking pictures. The member threatened: 'what will you do if I go on?' The staff member contained the attack in answering: 'probably nothing would actually happen, this would not be the point, and the transgression itself is'. Obviously my taking notes were my transgression. I had to stop it. Writing was my 'natural' defense vis-à-vis my anxiety in the group. For the sake of the relationship in the group I would have to give up my lifesaving defense which on the level of group interaction annoys, distracts, hurts other group members. I did. It worked. What a relief. I think such a moment is of great importance as a crossroad of falling neurotic, as a sticky point in the first-second generation conflict, as transgression point in the progressing of the development of the participants and the whole group" (Thomas Erdmann).

***

The Third Conference "This time in Germany" (Bad Segeberg)

"Milked with tears, milked with poison"

The possibility of having a conference in Germany was voiced right at the beginning of the whole Project. It was immediately dismissed with the argument that "the Israelis will not come" – it is hard enough for them to come to such a conference in Israel, so that to hold it in Germany will be too much. Five years later this was still true for some of the participants, but it was no longer inconceivable for a conference to take place in Germany.

A meeting of Israeli participants held two years after the second conference to consider this question came up with the recommendation that it was the right thing for it to be "this time in Germany". The Germans, however, had mixed feelings: on one hand they were thrilled to be confirmed as hosts, but on the other hand, the burden of hosting and ensuring that no harm will come again to the Jews in Germany was a heavy responsibility. Curiously enough, this conference had more Israeli participants than any of the conferences in Israel. Yet being in a conference in Germany affected the process in many unexpected ways as exemplified in what follows.

***

"Don't go with them, they killed your grandparents!"

"After the first two conferences on the theme: 'Germans and Israelis. The Past in the Present', which were held in Israel in 1994 and 1996, the third Nazareth conference was held in Germany. The Israeli colleagues' decision to accept the German group's invitation to hold the conference in Germany already sheds light on what was special about this third conference. Holding it in Germany was a risk for some participants of both nations. For some of the 21 Israeli participants, this conference would be their first visit in Germany ever. The German participants had the burdensome responsibility of being the hosts in a country where some of the guests' parents, grandparents and other family members had been murdered by the Germans. In the final plenary an Israeli participant reported very emotionally a telephone conversation he had had that morning with his mother, who lives in Israel. He told her he wanted to stay on for a few more days to spend some time with a German friend in Berlin. His mother's answer was: 'Don't do that, don't trust them, they killed your grandparents!' One could tell how painful it was for him to hurt his mother, to break the bonds of loyalty with her by visiting Berlin even more than he already had by participating in this Conference. On the other hand, one could also sense his resolve about taking this step and going to Berlin.

In my estimation, holding the conference in Germany had a far greater effect on unconscious dynamics and defences than the participants were able to review. For, meeting in Germany is inevitably bound up with the phenomenon which the Israeli participants referred to as 're-traumatization' in their first System Event group and discussed as such. For the Israelis, being in Germany necessarily means having to deal with the terror of the Holocaust inside –regardless of how they are received by the Germans today. And the Germans are inevitably confronted with this 're-traumatization', which makes their role as hosts more difficult. The sketched theme of the Germans' 'politeness' which was taken up with ambivalence by the Israelis fits in this context; as does the observation of one participant that during this Conference one spoke almost exclusively of 'the Israelis' and not about 'the Jews'. The re-traumatization is already stressful and dangerous enough for the Jewish conference participants. But it is obvious that even more far-reaching, vital risks, presumably more at an unconscious level, were at work because of the German conference site. I suspect that, unconsciously, a great deal of anxiety about a revival and *revitalization* of terror and destruction was at work: mortal anxiety, hatred and revenge on the Israeli side, fantasies about destruction and unbearable feelings of guilt on the German side. The right-wing radicals in Germany were a frequent topic. A German (female) participant who was out for a short walk came across a group of young skinheads who were giving each other the Nazi salute. She was terribly afraid that Israeli colleagues might come along. Coping with an internal revival of the Nazi terror means having to rely on protective defence mechanisms, one of which, a decisive one, I have already mentioned: the dialectics of a conference tradition that has grown and become familiar on the one hand favoured working on very far-reaching destructive fantasies and affects on a very personal level and, on the other, these personal relationships were one of the reasons why this destructiveness was NOT discharged primarily against the background of the Holocaust trauma, NOT, in other words, between '*the* Germans' and '*the* Jews.' The fear of such a re-enactment was understandably (and also protectively) very great, and consequently all of the Conference participants helped to keep such a revival within bounds" (Ursula Kreuzer-Haustein).

***

The System Event

Israelis

"Just before the System Event began, one of my German colleagues told me how anxious he was about the upcoming meeting. I, on the other hand, thought that my experience during the previous conference (Nazareth II) had somehow prepared me for what was to come. Only later did I realize how wrong I was.

The power struggle began at once, around chairs. The Israeli group was meeting in the room in which the Planeries were held, so that many of the chairs were still placed in a semicircle, one row behind the other. As people began to sit down, one participant – a 'newcomer' – said, 'Let's form a circle …' Immediately another participant – one of the 'veterans' – replied that the seating arrangement didn't bother her and that she felt quite comfortable with people sitting behind her: she saw no reason to rearrange the chairs.

It continued in the same way, and it was very clear from the outset that a struggle for leadership was under way. This struggle was fought especially (although not exclusively) by the 'veterans,' the majority of 'newcomers' not having any idea of what was going on. I was reminded of how I myself had felt in the first meeting of the System Event in Nazareth II, being at a loss to understand what was happening around me.

I knew that I did not want to be part of this power struggle. I hated the way that part of the group was fighting for leadership. Salvation suddenly appeared: two German participants came to ask whether we agreed to them sitting in as observers of the work in the Israeli group. Not to be outdone, the Israelis decided to send observers to the German group. I immediately volunteered: I had found a way out!

The scene in the German group was very different from what was going on in the Israeli group. Everything was very orderly; the proceedings were calm and precise. There seemed to be clear leadership, since everyone's comments seemed directed almost exclusively at one specific participant.

The topic in the German group was rules and procedures; they were discussing why the Germans were so rigid about rules and why they found it so difficult to be more flexible. Ironically, when the two German observers of the

Israeli group returned to make their report, the group went into an upheaval because the observers had not followed procedures, having returned a few minutes before the allotted 20 minutes. I wondered if anyone in the group saw the irony.

We Israeli observers took our cue at that point and returned to our own group, where I thought that the situation had deteriorated even further. The power struggles had worsened, and it felt as if insanity had broken loose. One participant was shrieking at the top of her voice: 'You don't understand: it's happening right now!' – 'it', being the Holocaust. Nobody seemed able to calm her down, and other participants had joined in her definition of reality. She had managed to convince the rest of the group that if they wanted to disperse into smaller groups, someone must, at all times, remain behind in the room originally used by the Israeli group – 'safeguarding the motherland.' (I told the participant who had volunteered to fulfill this task that she was a vestal virgin assigned to keep watch over the holy fire.) Only later in the conference, at a social event, when this participant's hilarious sense of humor became apparent was I reassured as to her sanity.

I found it totally absurd. If at first I had left to avoid being drawn into the power struggles, by now I wanted to get out of what I sensed was a situation bordering on insanity. At this point, about half the Israeli group chose to leave in order to join mixed groups. I joined one that was overwhelmingly German with only a small Israeli contingent. Only two of us in this small Israeli representation stayed in the group continuously; the others kept wandering between the 'original' Israeli home and the Diaspora.

In this mixed group a different kind of leadership developed, one much more to my taste, one derived not from taking power but rather from fulfilling needs. One of the German participants began to watch over the group; he became the gate-keeper, preventing anyone from disturbing the group processes. When participants from other groups came with messages or staff came to observe, he took it upon himself to go out, inquire what they wanted, and report back. Very naturally he became the group leader, having resorted neither to force nor the formation of coalitions, but rather by caring for the needs of the group.

From the vantage point of this mixed group, the Israeli group reminded us of the Jews in the Diaspora, always so busy fighting among them that they could not pay attention to anything around them.

In the course of the group, a German participant related how, when she came late to a meeting, another German participant had been worried that she might have committed suicide. This provoked my own concerns about the 'worrier' and, for the duration of the conference, I kept an eye of sorts on her.

These events made me realize that I had to a certain extent reenacted a part of my life. I had chosen to go out alone into the world over belonging to an insane family, where the insanity was too intense for me to be able to have a calming effect. My only choice was to leave; to stay sane, I had to give up belonging. That is also what brought me to Israel: less Zionism than the need to escape insanity (or to replace it with another kind of insanity). To draw a parallel: in Bad Segeberg, I left the Israeli group more because I needed to escape insanity than for any other reason.

If in Nazareth II the theme of *violence and killing* was, in my experience, predominant (it took place shortly after Rabin's assassination), and on German soil *insanity and potential suicide* were much more in the air" (Johana Gotesfeld).

***

Same process – the Israeli group in the System Event, another view:

"The leadership (of the Israeli group) that formed during the System Event was a collective one. It formed early, and survived massive resistance, and repeated challenge and assault. It coalesced gradually, was task oriented, was primarily compassionate, and eventually capable of acting firmly.

We hypothesize that the particular form of leadership that developed in the Israeli group was in response to the great tensions, and particular regressive tendencies that an Israeli-German conference on German soil induced.

The enormous fear of dictatorship, and particularly of a masculine phallic, ruthless one, that so strongly inhabited the conference, was an important factor in the specific formation that seemed to coalesce spontaneously. The group unconsciously mobilized the leadership team to take the form it did. There was no conscious overt discussion or decision about the composition of the leadership group, or the division of labor within it, nor were there any democratic procedures to nominate its members.

Throughout the System Event different parts or sub-groups of the Israeli membership launched repeated attacks on the leadership. The leadership was accused of being ruthless and totalitarian (Bolshevik), oblivious to individual needs, insensitive, intolerant of diversity, and overly goal oriented or concrete.

The analysis of the leadership's mode of operation clearly shows that its central role as it crystallized under the very specific conditions of the German-Israeli conference was first and foremost the containment of anxiety. In the face of near panic and a danger of fragmentation no setting of goals, or mobilization to productive action was possible unless attention was given to holding the group together. Members who felt overwhelmed, excluded, hostile and combative or helpless and lost were attended.

... The collective leadership as it formed in the third German-Israeli conference was a group of second generation members of four sub-groups: (1) the Israelis of German origin; (2) Holocaust refugees; (3) Holocaust survivors; (4) Ashkenazi immigrants from other parts of the Jewish Diaspora. Trauma – uprooting, loss, physical and mental torment – was to some extent or another, part of the heritage of each of these groups. They all saw the destruction of the world they had come from.

This leadership was unconsciously mobilized to represent the entire Israeli membership.

Resistance to Leadership

Anxiety was present from the very beginning. It was exacerbated, and reached near panic when delegates from the German group entered with a list of subjects they wanted the Israeli group to consider.

... The Israeli membership would not allow an active and assertive leadership to thrive; implicitly authority was granted only for containment and empathy. It was as though the Israeli group was a patient that felt too fragile, and was thus able to tolerate only supportive rather than insight-oriented therapy.

Still, a leadership did form. It formed and coalesced during the first two sessions of the System Event. It did so in the face of ever mounting anxiety, and an enormous threat of breakdown.

The prevailing basic assumption during those initial sessions, and possibly throughout the entire System Event, was 'fight/flight', the members either planning their escape, or protesting angrily, and opposing any suggestion of productive action. Anxiety peaked quite quickly, and confusion reigned immediately; the group pulled in different directions; it threatened to spit, nay, to splinter! Some members wanted to stay put, freeze while vigilantly guarding their place. Others were eager to flee, rush out without even having a flimsy agenda.

On a deeper level though, the situation in the Israeli group was an instantaneous recreation in the room of the pre-Holocaust and Holocaust condition of the Jews.

We hypothesize that the precipitous entry of the German delegates in the first session of the System Event was experienced as the unprepared for and sudden German invasion (or Nazi seizure of power), and epitomized German efficiency. In the third session, the initiative of some Israeli members to integrate the experience thus far, and the call to divide into groups was associated with an internal seizure of power by community leaders (Judenrath); it triggered deep suspicion, caused instant splintering, and was thus a repetition of the panic of masses faced with the threat of uprooting, deportation and annihilation.

Let us now quote some relevant excerpts from the hypothesis as it was formulated between the second and third sessions of the System Event: 'The encounter between Israelis and Germans on German soil implies and activates a sense of approaching catastrophe ... On the membership level the re-traumatization occurred when ambassadors from the German group presented themselves to the Israeli group. This was perceived as a chaotic invasion, and reverberated in the Israeli group, thus creating parallel chaos, brutality and paralysis. There was an inability to allow leadership to emerge, the hypothesis being that any leadership would be experienced either as cruel dictatorship, or as impotent, leading to uncontained anarchy...'

To sum up the now supported observation that in the Israeli group there was a dire need for leadership, but a vehement/desperate resistance to its formation, we would like to postulate that this conflict was an unconscious expression in the here and now of the group's both far and recent historic experience with leadership. For Jews who were directly or indirectly connected to the Holocaust, for immigrants who after the catastrophe were supposed to accept a leadership they had no energy, language or social skills to evaluate or fathom, as well as for Israeli Jews who had only several years ago experienced the inconceivable traumatic assassination of a democratically elected leader, leadership was laden with life-threatening frightful associations, and freedom with the danger of repeating history. For potential followers it aroused associations of impotence, absenteeism, betrayal, chaos, ruthlessness, and abandonment; for potential leaders it evoked feelings of self-torment, loneliness, heart-rending dilemmas, and a real threat to ones existence" (Ilana Litvin and Izhak Mendelson).

***

A German perspective of the same event

"I want to describe my experience of the Systems Event: aggression seems to have been acted out within each participants group: within the German and Israeli group.

From the beginning of the first Plenary there was a sense of an impending catastrophe, a menacing fear of something dreadful to happen. I did not fear retaliation from the Israeli side; I expected to hear and listen to very sad memories about the experience of the victims. As a German who has heard these life stories for the first time only since I moved to live in England, I am aware they have not been heard and listened to enough in Germany, certainly not during my time in Germany. My fear was for the Israeli group, what might happen to them and that not in the sense of any gross violation that could happen. I feared what I know about how the past, certain attitudes continue to be lived out in Germans in the present: their lack of empathy, the inability to mourn, a general egocentricity in the German character, their defensive armor, the acting out of projective identifications.

However, perhaps it was not surprising to find that the German participants attending this conference came with greater sensitivities than most Germans one meets in ordinary life in Germany. In my experience the Germans were trying to be 'good' to the Israelis, aggression seemed a taboo. However, once the groups were separated into their own national group, the German group split and fragmented into arguments about politics (inner German: our relationship to authority; German-Israeli: which language do we speak in: our German language or English: the language we shared with the Israeli group). The German group was in disarray; it was paralyzed, disabled. It gave the impression of acting out destructive aggression which led participants to attack each other, rather than exchange and communicate about different views in a rational manner. In the guise of sophisticated political arguments something more primitive, catastrophic was acted out which could not be recognized, named and thought about. Only in the presence of two consultants did the group emerge from its impasse and began to function sufficiently that we could focus on our task of establishing and developing relationships to the Israelis and see how we could come together. A messenger was sent over as observer to the Israelis, and an Israeli messenger came to observe the German group in their proceedings. Eventually we found, when we asked the Israeli group for their suggestions about topics for dividing the groups into sub groups; they quickly came up with a list of topics they wanted to discuss with us. These topics were essential to all of us, but the German group had not been able to formulate any of them themselves. Instead they had acted out splitting attacks on their awareness of an unbearable reality related to the German past which incapacitated them.

The Systems Event then continued on the basis Subgroups which formed to discuss these topics.

A similar process of the group being taken over by primitive psychotic mechanisms under the guise of politics as we have seen in the German group seems to have also happened to the Israeli group while they were on their own. Personally I have not been present but the experience conveyed to us by some Israelis participants who left their group suggests this was so. But there was a significant difference. Some Israelis experienced what happened in their group as a takeover by a subgroup which was seen as a political party. In a similar guise of politics it seems this group acted out a more organized defense against the anxieties in their group: an acute paranoid anxiety that must have been stirred up in the Israeli group as a result of coming to Germany.

I want to describe the Systems Event from the perspective of having been part of a fairly large group of both German and Israelis (a sizable group of Israelis most of whom refused to be involved in what was happening in their Israeli group).

This German-Israeli group came together under the topic: *Identifications with the perpetrators and the victims.* In this group we had the remarkable experience of trying to concentrate our minds on what we felt was the most essential topic of the conference, and meet the 'others' so that we may face it together. In our attempt to concentrate on our experience in this group we found we were being invaded by reports of disturbing events in the Israeli group which had a disabling effects on us, in disrupting our attempts to think about our own topic. We felt distracted, drawn into the excitement of what was happening there which was experienced by the Israeli members of our group as mad, a hijacking of the agenda of our conference by a political party. An interesting parallel: both national groups, once left on their own got involved in political arguments which evaded the real issues and agenda of our conference. At one point the staff sent a message. Once the group was on its own again and tried to take up and think about the message, there was no one in the group who could remember what had been said, except that we were aware it was a message central to our topic and concern. In a common effort the group members then put together the staff's interpretation from bits several members of the group had heard and remembered. The hypothesis goes as follows: *'Participants have put themselves into a painful situation by coming to this conference, which can be experienced as cruel. This leads to greater dependency on staff for containment, along with fears and disappointment of fantasies about the insufficiency of staff resources. The fearful fantasies may have to do with unexpected, powerful changes in one's sense of identity and the giving up of precious parts of identity, such as the role of the victim (for the Israelis) or the guilt of perpetrators (for the Germans).'* In the course of this group effort the group process and our discussion became more focused. We realized how we had been disabled and distracted by the more powerful events in the Systems Event. This seemed to enable the group to begin to discuss our topic which both, Israelis and Germans in this group seemed to feel was closer to the real agenda of our conference. We called in a consultant for assistance and without much discussion agreed on one particular consultant who represented neither group, she represented neutrality; a position, the analytic position, we found ourselves in a new situation that enabled to make use of the group in a new way. In the presence of this consultant we began to formulate what we were trying to think about in our group. She listened with interest, was moved and impressed about the maturity of what we were trying to think about, she expressed her surprise that our efforts seemed to have disappeared in the System Event. As we had not kept in contact with the staff, our struggles and efforts were unknown to the staff. She interpreted we were like children without parents who were trying to be adults ourselves. The System Event came to its end not long after this intervention. Before it ended some important themes emerged: two German members of the group expressed their struggle with internal objects which seemed to condemn them, 'you are guilty', accused them of having murdered 'my parents, grandparents'. This came up in the group as if they were hearing this as coming from the Israeli members of the group who in reality had not said this. Once it became clear that they cannot actually be accused and condemned for having killed any of our Israeli friends members of their families, this came as a revelation to them as they seemed to believe they are actually guilty of these crimes, a belief they could not bear and felt very conflicted about. Another theme, perhaps the theme that came closest to the most difficult aspect of the topic of our group in the SE was brought up by a German participant who was half Jewish, and had a Jewish mother who she had experienced as behaving like a Nazi towards her. She was able to convey to the group her despair about this experience. There was no more time to process any of this further. However, the despair was such, something needed to be done with it. It was instantaneously turned into a bitter joke running like *'if a German and a Jew are coming together, all you can do is commit suicide'*. Actually, she had meant that if they come together in oneself – there is no chance. Walking away from this Systems Event we had a short lived laugh about this joke, knowing it was not a joke. Had there been more time, the despair could have been processed with the prospect of a better outcome. It has been most unfortunate that this joke ended up being put on the conference notice board. Out of context, open to misunderstandings that could have been catastrophic.

It made very clear, we ended the System Event feeling that we needed a new conference and that we were only just beginning" (Hella Ehlers).

***

"The meeting between Germans and Israelis on German soil for the Israelis implies and activates a sense of an approaching catastrophe. Anxiety was growing, some began to tremble. The wish of the Germans to come together with Israelis in working groups was experienced as a destructive invasion, creating in the Israeli group 'chaos, brutality and paralysis'. A group of the Israelis tried to 'disentangle from this repetitious paranoid position' by developing a working hypothesis that they wrote down and gave all participants with the suggestion to discuss it with the others, especially with the Germans. An interchange during one of the Conference Plenaries between staff-members was experienced by the Israelis as brutal and gave them the feeling that the 'centre cannot hold'. The version of the working hypothesis that I give here is in incomplete form, yet it was part of the System Event and influenced it. There was no discussion that followed it. It seemed that a need for regulating affects reduced the energy. Finally there was an intervention by the staff, giving their only hypothesis. The staff's Working Hypothesis was read out by different staff-members at the same moment in all working groups.

The staff gave the following hypothesis: 'Participants have put themselves into a painful situation by coming to this conference, which can be experienced as cruel. This leads to greater dependency on staff for containment, along with fears and disappointment of fantasies about the insufficiency of staff resources. The fearful fantasies may have to do with unexpected, powerful changes in one's sense of identity and the giving up of precious parts of identity, such as the role of the victim (for the Israelis) or the guilt of perpetrators (for the Germans).

For me, the staff had expressed something unbelievable: the role of victims for the Israelis and the guilt of perpetrators for the Germans should be 'worthy' parts of the own identity! This is difficult to accept. The hypothesis suggested the idea that parts of this identity could be given up. But if so then what then? Wouldn't that mean for the Jewish group to dis-identify from the role of victim and for the non-Jewish group to dis-identify from the guilt of perpetrator? Wouldn't that mean to separate in a more deep way from parents who, not only in the world of inner objects but often also in real life have to be the space for our own anxiety or wishes for destruction? Where to put these feelings when the space for it would be lost? What could be the consequences for oneself as well as for the meeting with the others? Isn't one that is touching a taboo in danger of becoming a taboo?

Fearful questions might follow from this hypothesis, and many more became possible" (Eva-Maria Staudinger).

***

An Israeli staff member's perspective

"The atmosphere in the System Event is typically quite intense and charged. It can sway from euphoric excitement and manic feelings of being powerful and 'doing things' to utter confusion, depressive passivity and dangerous resignation. It is the event most prone and available for the actual reenactment of unconscious themes and contents.

In the two Nazareth conferences, the German group was seen as efficient, active and powerful, while the Israelis seemed passive, helpless and resigned. An intervention by a consultant in the first Nazareth conference was that 'while the Germans were marching, the Jews sat and debated what to do.' In Bad Segeberg, the Israeli group – quite unlike the previous conferences – became extremely active. There was a leadership struggle in it, resulting in a powerful group taking over, with a sense of mission and purpose, of knowing how to play the game and 'get it right.' It created resentment and disunity among the Israelis. Some of them experienced this as a Fascist take over, with which they could not identify. Several Israelis left the big group, to create or join other groups. The first to leave was an Israeli man of the pre-war generation, who wanted to create a group together with Germans to investigate events in Germany from 1933 to 1945. For some time, he was a group of one, wandering around in disarray, like a refugee in flight, carrying plastic bags with his belongings. Seven or eight Germans, who provided him with shelter and protection, later joined him. The name adopted by this group was 'The German Catastrophe.' An Israeli woman came to the Staff in a stormy, highly charged emotional state. She wondered if the staff knew what was actually going on. She felt confused, angry and disoriented. She could not see what all this had to do with her grandparents who were murdered in Auschwitz.

The German group, which in previous conferences was quite active, was more passive and subdued this time. Acting orderly and democratically, it was beset and plagued by procedural debates. The group stayed in this paralysis until it asked for and received consultation, which freed it up. It then formed several subgroups, which were joined by Israeli members. The titles these groups took were instructive: 'On Violence and Sentimentality' (all women); 'Lack of Safety'; 'The Murdered and the Murderers'; and 'The German Catastrophe' mentioned before.

Throughout the conference in Bad Segeberg, in sharp contradistinction to

Nazareth I and II, there were repeated defensive enactments, at first totally unconscious, of German incompetence. This took on a number of faces: The Germans idealized the competence of the Israelis, and unjustly downgraded their own. There was evidence (e.g., in the Small Study Groups) of the Germans 'lobotomizing' themselves, cutting off their heads and brains, their capacity to think and feel. They often complained of their inability to think and to use their intellect, an experience bordering on madness. This was linked to an observed German tendency to come off as inadequate, incompetent and tongue-tied in international meetings. A tremendous amount of shame and guilt accompanied this. It was also evident that the Germans longed for their Jewish colleagues and counterparts. They felt deprived, severely handicapped and lacking without them. They longed desperately for the taste of the Jewish breast and milk, of which they had ridded themselves" (H. Shmuel Erlich).

***

A German staff member's perspective

"In Bad Segeberg, an enormous anxiety about the Germans spread very soon in the Israeli group. The decision in favour of a German conference site had been made in Israel. It was clear to all of us that a conference on German soil would raise the Israeli participants' fear of the Germans enormously, but also the oppressiveness because of possibly betraying their own families. When I was able to witness the Israeli group in the second System Event session, I was impressed by the concreteness of the anxiety-related convictions. Some of them were trembling. They experienced themselves as being completely unprotected and without leadership. They would be going into the Holocaust, they said, if they went next door to the Germans. Fear of annihilation and degradation were massively present. Kathy Pogue-White, our associate director, a black professor and analyst from New York, gave the interpretation as a consultant that the group had projected its own Israeli Fascism, which after all existed at home, onto the Germans next door. That was the reason for the tremendous anxiety. The interpretation was so friendly and matter-of-fact that it worked. The group was able to work better. It formulated a number of themes to invite and engage with the Germans.

I don't know today whether the interpretation correctly corresponded to the phenomenon that we experienced with that group. Today I suspect that it was a matter of becoming aware of a collective Israeli symptom, a traumatic awareness and realization *(Vergegenwärtigung)* of the Holocaust that the group could not defend itself against, which also honours the dead in order never to forget them, and which expects the annihilating mentality to come back and wants to prevent it. Perhaps the two interpretations are complementary.

Two of the working groups, *'The catastrophe of their conscience'* and *'Cruelty, omnipotence and dominance in the conference'*, offered the following hypothesis in the fourth SE session.

'The encounter between Israelis and Germans on German soil implies and activates a sense of approaching catastrophe. There was an inability to allow leadership to emerge, the hypothesis being that any leadership might be experienced either as a cruel dictatorship or as impotent, leading to uncontained anarchy. This creates a situation where any form of leadership is experienced as using power in the worst sense of the word. Part of the anarchy is the perverse obliteration of differences, between power and weakness and roles of victim and persecutor.

In order to disentangle from this repetitious paranoid position, we need the German group to talk and see how they deal with their own catastrophe'.

The following staff hypothesis then summarized the dynamics of the whole system event:

Participants have put themselves into a painful situation by coming to this conference, which can be experienced as cruel. This leads to greater dependency on staff for containment, along with fears and disappointment fantasies about the insufficiency of staff resources. These fearful fantasies may have to do with unexpected, powerful changes in one's sense of identity and the giving up of precious parts of identity, such as the role of the victim (for the Israelis) or the guilt of perpetrators (for the Germans).

It was the first time that such a central idea for change, and the anxiety about it, came up in the framework of the conferences. I found it extraordinarily important. It made the conference dynamics understandable and had a liberating effect. Especially the second part of the interpretation, I felt, took up developments from the end of the second conference in Nazareth, where a German feeling of hopelessness and collective paralysis was taking shape about not being part of humanity. This peculiar paralysis can be regarded as a collective symptom, as the accepted mark of Cain. At the third conference, for the first time, this German paralysis that occurs in the presence of other nations was put into question in the form of an interpretation, as an annoying refusal (from the non-Germans' point of view) to work together in a certain sense. That went too fast for me, but I was thankful that this peculiar phenomenon got its right to exist as a collective symptom for the first time. I think that more research on this is absolutely necessary before it can be included in the work as a secretly valued but extremely painful part of our own identity in the large group, and can perhaps be dealt with" (Hermann Beland).

***

IV.5   The Danger/Fear of False Reconciliation

"I am not my father, but his daughter."

Unlike other conferences having to do with the Holocaust, the Primary Task of these conferences is described in the brochure in the following way:
   "To provide opportunities for participants to explore how feelings and fantasies about 'German-ness' and 'Israeli-ness'/'Jewish-ness' influence relations within and between the two groups in the conference".
   The aim as stated is about "exploring" and not about reconciliation. Nonetheless, there was a wish for reconciliation as well as the fear of it being a "false reconciliation" that says: "Let's put the Holocaust behind us once and for all and just be human beings". On the other hand, it was clear that viewing the conference from this viewpoint was seen as "obscene".

***

"I experienced 'them' (the Germans) as if coming 'without parents'. Some denied their parents, some tried to analyze them some hated them overtly but without any identification. I cannot 'buy' as yet this kind of merchandise. It seems that they grew up in harshness, aggression, at time in evil and without mercy. They came to us for the good parents, to get warm near the

Jewish heart. Their harsh parents were not there with them, though they were hidden in them and their deeds. Here and there they would peep out but than as a wild herb that is to be uprooted, so that the garden will be nice again.

I see a possible contact between us thus: if they can come to us not in a pose of the atoned-one seeking forgiveness, it will be better for them and maybe they will achieve something. For as far as I am concerned, reconciliation it will not elicit" (Robi Friedman).

***

"In addition to the fear of reviving the Holocaust trauma in Germany, a completely different, but nonetheless related anxiety was also at work: the fear of a *false reconciliation*. This could happen if parts of the victim identity and parts of the perpetrator identity were put in question. This danger is also part of an interpretation that the staff injected into all system event groups on the third day: *'Participants have put themselves into a painful situation by coming to this conference, which can be experienced as cruel. This leads to greater dependency on staff for containment, along with fears and disappointment of fantasies about the insufficiency of staff resources. The fearful fantasies may have to do with unexpected, powerful changes in one's sense of identity and the giving up of precious parts of identity, such as the role of the victim (for the Israelis) or the guilt of perpetrators (for the Germans).'*

The risk of false reconciliation, of putting the Holocaust behind us once and for all, was already a central theme during the first Nazareth conference.

This danger has grown due to the relationships that have taken shape among colleagues and on a personal level. During this conference, there were many different scenes in which this danger was present in the atmosphere. What all of these scenes had in common was the difficulty of striking a balance between the wish for just individual 'human' relationships between Germans and Israelis and the certainty that, ultimately, such a 'normality' is not possible and also not desirable: During one session in a system event group with German and Israeli participants, a German participant tells about how broken her father was when he came back from the war. There is a wish in the room for the Israelis to say something about this, something conciliatory perhaps. The Israeli colleague who told about the telephone conversation with his mother during the final plenary session ('don't go with them, they have killed your grandparents'), replies that he had grown up with his mother's absolute irreconcilability of never speaking with the Germans again. The German female participant put him in a difficult position, he said. What should he say? On a human level he could develop feelings of compassion, but for him the Holocaust was 'unforgivable'. *The Germans' wish for reconciliation, perhaps even forgiveness from the Israelis, comes up over and over again, an irresolvable situation.* It is also manifested in the wish of some German participants to belong to the Jews, idealizing them, fantasizing them as exclusively good objects. These fantasies and wishes prove to be, among other things, the expression of a wish to be relieved of guilt, as the wish to be on the 'right' side, the victim side, and to be rid of the historical responsibility once and for all, which, for some German participants, is mixed with a feeling of guilt that weighs on them personally. At the same time, the primitive picture of the 'good Jew', of the Jew equipped with special knowledge, is used to ward off hostile affects against the Jews: *The idealization distracts from anti-Semitic, destructive inclinations.* The phenomenon, often described in the literature on anti-Semitism, of the dialectic of 'philo-Semitism and anti-Semitism ... a stubborn idealization and devaluation' vis-à-vis Jews, is manifested here as well. At first glance, one German female participant's dream holds the described yearning to belong to the Jews: in the dream she sees *a gathering of Jews, some of them wearing yarmulkes, and she wakes up in tears because she feels totally excluded and that she does not belong*. On second glance, several details and associations reveal the underlying inclination towards clichés and anti-Semitic elements: A Jewish family in this dream reminds her of a fleetingly known, very unpleasant, ascetic-miserly Swabian family; the Jews in the dream are meeting in a synagogue, but the synagogue is the 'Deutsche Bank'.

The danger of false reconciliation, however, was never so great that the boundary line between perpetrator and victim disappeared. The first system-event setting takes place on the second day: Israelis and Germans meet in their separate national groups. The Germans work on some themes that they want to discuss together with Israeli colleagues, the theme of the 'ugly German', for example, or the question of whether during this conference there is a shift in the aggressiveness between Germans and Israelis to the relations between German and Israelis amongst themselves. Towards the end of the first system-event session, the Germans send an ambassador to the Israelis and present their proposed themes. The Israelis reply that they need more time, they are dealing with similar themes, but with much sharper formulations. The Germans now try to make their themes more precise, but are almost exclusively preoccupied with the Israeli colleagues. This gives rise to impatience, perhaps also anxiety, over whether any cooperation will take place at all. From this hectic atmosphere, an ambassador is sent to the Israelis again during the next system event session with the mission of listening to them as a guest for half an hour and then coming back to the German group. This German colleague comes back 10 minutes earlier than agreed and intensifies the Germans' agitation and anxiety with the keyword 're-traumatisation.' The Israelis, as he reports, are discussing risks of a false fraternization, resulting in romantic reaction formation, one proposed theme, for example, is 'schmaltz and kitsch'. The Israelis feel 'abused' by our friendliness, he says. All of a sudden, not just anxiety and mistrust but also wishes to barricade themselves are noticeable in the German group. The two consultants who have been consulted – a German woman and an Israeli – also interpret the process and atmosphere as an expression of the wish for a protective wall; it is also obvious that the Germans did not want to form a group leader for their various proposed themes because this kind of leadership might be too dangerous vis-à-vis the Jews. The theme of retraumatization is also discussed further in the small groups; one participant says he does not want to be retraumatizing as the host, nor is he. Some Israelis answer these statements with the simple fact: Being here in Germany is always retraumatizing for us.

So, the boundary between Germans and Israelis was always in effect, the danger of false fraternalization, reaction formation (*'schmaltz and kitsch'* was the theme of one of the groups) existed nonetheless and was repeatedly answered with counter movements. That could also be felt very clearly when some Israelis, especially those who had still been born in Germany, spoke about their love for Germany: the culture, the apple cake, the greenery, the lakes and much more. This love for Germany which could be felt upset some Germans and confronted them with the question that repeatedly perplexed them, why the Nazis killed the German Jews, who loved Germany so much. Whenever the Jews speak about their love for Germany during this conference, it is always clearly recognizable that it is a matter of *their love for Germany and not for the Germans.* An Israeli participant in a small group is enthused about the many lakes in the Holstein lowland plain and says she wished she could take a lake back with her to Israel. Another Israeli adds: '*A lake from Germany without the Germans*'" (Ursula Kreuzer-Haustein).

***

"There may be hope for the present and future in the possibility of changing perspectives. It is not a search for symmetry. I think this is a false hope, an illusionary belief some Germans still adhere to. It is of the same order as the belief that ordinary Germans are not guilty of anything because they have not killed anyone. This lie is a continuation of the old lie from the past, we didn't know about the Holocaust. It is this web of lies Germans are still caught up in which prevents them to see what they really have done and emerge from the past which is the poison we still carry around with ourselves. There is something deadly about the way this is living, a constant present, and the difficulty the Germans will face in emerging from it.
Quote: Ernst Jandl

In Accord with Old Custom
No one after all
wanted it
everyone after all did it
this sounds like a lie
and it is one
(Hella Ehlers)

Nach altem Brauch
Keiner schließlich
hat es gewollt
jeder schließlich hat es getan
das hört sich an wie Lüge
und ist es auch"

***

"My perception of what happens in our country with view to our past has been sharpened, and I have begun to detect the defence against guilt and shame even in my (and others') upright criticism of signs of present anti-Semitism in our country – it is such a relief for me/us to detect it in others! It is so difficult to face my/our own destructiveness" (Veronika Grueneisen).

***

"This is my little victory over what happened there. Destruction does not win in a place where people fight to find the human in the other, and who can be more 'other' than Germans and Jews? This fight is worthy of having presence in the written word as well. The same words they used as an instrument for distorting reality can now be used to express what really (in my own subjective reality) happened between the Germans and Jews in Nazareth I" (Yoram Hazan).

***

"In this conference there were other, freer, less painful contacts with Israeli colleagues as well. There was something very touching even, when a very old – maybe the oldest Jewish-Israeli participant, hugged me – not reconciling or forgiving way (compare H. Klein 1983/92) but as that of a fellow human being.

But, I felt so shaken and shamed and thin-skinned as well, because of the contact with my possible guilt; with the side of me that could possibly be a culprit, which I had to draw back from it. Further work on that aspect would be needed for the time being and from that understanding.

My experience in the Review and Application Group only reinforced my inner situation.

At first I had to fight with not finding a theme to work on in the group; at the time it was not possible even to talk about not being able to find a theme and what does that mean. Today, however, I understand that it was not possible for me to fantasize about a 'future', a future with my inner objects" (Thea Wittmann).

***

"We, the German members of this group, have to face the fact, that after all that Germans in the time of Nazism made themselves responsible of the holocaust we can't expect to be recognized by the Israelis colleagues as individuals. That is how it is. But we would like to state, that we do not accept a generalized guilt, but only that guilt, for which one is *personally* responsible for.'

I felt fundamentally relieved by this, with the simple consequence: *I am not my father, but his daughter*" (Jutta Matzner-Eicke).

***

"I got some friends in the conference. I was invited to come again to Israel, but during the coffee break I had to learn that my invitation to them to come to Germany was refused definitely. For many Israelis a visit to Germany still is impossible. After Bad Segeberg I understand this and I was sad and ashamed about my 'simple question'.

When I started the conference, I was hoping to overcome a gap, sometimes eager in revealing our German history and its denial. When I returned, I was much more composed, realizing this huge gap and the strain to overcome it. My senses concerning denial were sharpened – but my respect for those, who can't face this history grew, too: it is a very personal decision and it may be hard.

So, with a sigh, I want to say, that we need a lot of further conferences" (Eva Mack).

***

"I think, there may be an answer to Mira's comment 'beyond asymmetry', it requires changing perspectives, and there may be hope for the present and future in it. The search for symmetry is a false hope, an illusionary belief some Germans still adhere to. It is of the same order as the belief ordinary Germans are not guilty of anything because they have not killed anyone. This lie is a continuation of the old lie from the past, 'we didn't know about the Holocaust'. It is this web of lies Germans are still caught up in which prevents them to see what they really have done and emerge from the past which is the poison we still carry around with ourselves" (Hella Ehlers).

***

IV.6 By way of Outcome – Getting out from the Imprisonment of the Past

"From Blood to Tears, from Tears to Words"

What is the outcome of these conferences? This is a difficult question. Is it the learning of the members? Is it the chance to "get out from the imprisonment of the past"? Or is it the implementation of the learning and its application to the wider professional or social community? The answer is: All of these and also none of them. Different participants have different expectations and varying definitions of what should be the expected outcome for the participants and for the project as a whole, as is apparent from what follows. The main tension is between the wish to "move from blood to tears and from tears to words" and the fear that any movement and change will mean betraying the parents and victims. Yet from one conference to the next we could see a development. There was a move from the initial strong need to tell "my story" to the other, who serves as a witness, to an inner space that is "beyond the story". This place, which is characterized by greater freedom, allowed for moving away from stereotyped roles. For example, the Jews could also be aggressive and perpetrators and Germans could be victims.

***

"I think that most of the participants at the three conferences would agree that the conferences achieved much of what was formulated as the primary task. A few hundred central experiences were gained, were and are individually valid and collectively important. Each and every one of us there, both groups, have had experiences and gained insights that contained deeper perceptions of identity for both peoples as subjective experience, which, as one Nazareth I participant put it, was like a trip to a place where none of us had ever been before, with the only partners possible for getting there. These experiences radiate to other individuals and groups.

If, in spite of my limited angle of perception and perhaps prematurely, I am trying to describe some of the changes on both sides, which fairly obviously were *collectively structured*, then those were the following:

➤ Sharing the family histories on both sides put an end to the collectively held prejudices about the families and relatives of the other nation. The developmental damages, Jewish and German, respectively, that everyone heard about put an end to the impersonal and stereotypical notions about 'the' children of the Nazis and 'the' children of the survivors, about 'the' Germans, 'the' Israelis.

➤ There was a diminishing of paranoid anxiety about inevitable blame and

collective retaliation among many German participants and an increase in the recognition of German motives and acts that led to the Holocaust.
- There was a liberation from the family-related obligation among some Israelis of having to hate the Germans as Nazis.
- There were friendships with a great deal of attentiveness to conflicting experiences and unbridgeable gaps that were not denied.
- The acknowledgement of a collective German symptom was achieved, which becomes virulent in the presence of other peoples and reflects the responsibility for the Holocaust, of not being entitled to normal social competence (Cain syndrome)
- The integration of German roots of many Israeli participants was initiated.

I find that these are extraordinarily great and important changes which, triggered by the group-dynamic experiential knowledge of such group conferences, only became possible through the presence of people of both nations" (Hermann Beland).

***

"When, with a week's distance, I had reached a conclusion about this conference, what stood out was that old encrusted behavioral patterns were shattered. In the difficult dialogues between the German and Israeli participants, it was possible to experience the inconsistent, the indistinct, the hardened, the injurious, and to bring the conversation around to these things. And in this connection, that was very liberating. We always and again achieved openness and skepticism" (Angelika Zitzelsberger-Schlez)

***

"Evaluation of a conference has to be largely subjective. Did the process of moving from event to event *feel* right? Did it provide members with opportunities to engage with the primary task? Did it enable them to learn? Some of the answers to these questions may appear in other contributions to this volume. One other question is: Did the staff learn? Speaking for myself, I certainly did" (Eric Miller).

***

"Changing identities is destabilizing the picture we have about ourselves, about the other, about the world; it brings a feeling of crisis, questions full of fear and a lot of worry. For instance, some of the Israelis became worried when they noticed it wasn't strange for them to be enjoying the lovely scent of apple cake, nor when they noticed the rain brought fresh green to the trees, which produced in the Israelis a feeling of longing for such colours. 'Oh, if it could be possible,' a colleague from Israel said at dinner, 'to take home only one of these beautiful lakes.' Others felt the opposite: 'Germany is beautiful, the Germans are ugly.'

The freedom to review the past from my own perspective and in my own time gives me the freedom to not be imprisoned by the past. Both can open up a way for a future, however uncertain. To look at this helps in recognizing the difference between the 'other' and my fantasies about him/her. This releases me from the imprisonment of fantasies and releases the 'other' from the world of my inner objects – I become empty and I don't need to project my inner objects on the 'other' any longer – it is a purifying process and I am not stuck. Then, and only then, are both (the other and myself) free to choose relationship with one another, or not. To come to this point, we have to share experiences because we need the 'other' to show us ourselves 'other'. This helps us all realize our participation in collective, cultural obligations, and helps us to see the ways in which we imprison ourselves, risking the passing on of the silence to the next generation. The cultural and historical obligations, for instance, of eternal mourning and hatred on one side and that of eternal guilt and never understanding/knowing on the other side. To share experiences can help to transport myths, taboos and fantasies to a place in reality.

False reconciliation serving nothing else than defence, would have been an 'obscene' undertaking. The conference left me with an unexpected hope: the hope for success on both sides for us and for them to be free of projecting our inner objects on the other, and that it would be possible to look into the eyes of the other without being flooded by our fantasies about him/her. At the same time this is a nearly impossible demand because to do this we would have to give up the roles that have been 'worthy' parts of our identity. As long as the past is not allowed to have room in our remembrance, and as long as the past is recognized as different from the present, then the past will have a much stronger influence than the present will in determining our identity. The past will never end in the sense of being over/finished, although some of us wish it so – it is a process! But if we do not give the present a chance, we will never have a future which can be experienced as different from the past.

The conference in Bad Segeberg is now part of the past like the conferences I and II in Nazareth. Looking back, questions appear; questions about the success or failure of the conferences. Did anything happen in self, life or work 'that can be linked to the conference?' A staff-member posted this question on the Internet, where a web site for conference members had been established.

What changed for me in self, life and work is first of all the question of responsibility. Those who lived in and have been part of the past are responsible for the past. Those living in the present are responsible for the present. To demand a responsibility for the past paralyses people – it is not possible to change the past. It is good enough to feel responsible for the present, where we have the ability to change things. And, if the poison of the Nazi-idea is still working, then we all, being part of the present, are responsible for it. And, if we want to change something, then we have to feel responsible for change and this will give us the ability to affect change.

There are several phenomena in Germany, which are recognized as current effects of the poison of the Nazi-idea. The conference revealed some of them. I will mention two:

My first example is taken from our psychoanalytic community. If we open our eyes, we can see that *Nazi-time in Germany is not necessarily a self-evident part of the psychoanalytic process.* When it is described or published about patients, that part of our history is usually not the subject of the report, nor is it considered an integral part of the patients disorder, or as a fact giving any difficulties to the psychoanalyst's own process. There is no systematical discussion about technical problems, about countertransference for instance. We pretend that nothing is missing. Excluding Nazi-time seems to be the usual course. Only a few courageous psychoanalysts seem to feel responsible for that subject and publish about it. The exceptions, if they publish at all, do so regarding clinical studies And, usually they have to find a special publication outside the mainstream. Looking at clinical case-studies, it is impressive what tiny little details interest us. Not, that they are not important, but there is a special disproportion between our interest in tiny details and our interest in what really is not a tiny detail; Nazi-time and its effect in the souls of our patients.

The destruction in war and Nazi-time was immense and it is unthinkable that there should be no destructive effects in the souls of those who survived – on both sides. And, it is impossible to think that these destructive effects have not been passed on to the next and following generations. Broken houses were built up again; broken souls have been forgotten. And, as long as Nazi-time is not a self-evident part of the psychoanalytic process in Germany, we leave ourselves and our patients alone with those parts of broken souls which refer back to this part of our common history. We can change this if we want to, but we have to realize it as a real and necessary phenomenon that requires changing, and we have to feel responsible for that change.

My second examples are the Neo-Nazis in Germany. At the least, we are against them. At the least, we call for police or take part in demonstrations against them. But, we don't talk to them. We don't want to realize that they are our children, coming out of our midst and that their hatred is a message to us. They are young people with no containment for their hatred, without hope, fluctuating between delusion of grandiosity and weakness. They show us a broken identity and we leave them alone. *If we want to feel responsible for that ugly phenomenon in our society, we can change something.*

There must be a reason for refusing to talk to our patients about Nazi-time and its effect in their souls and for refusing to talk to Neo-Nazis. We can recognize it as something well known. *We don't talk to them as our parents did not talk to us.* In both cases there is a lack of readiness to feel responsible. That lack has to do with the common history. We know by doing our psychoanalytic work that we have to offer ourselves to the patient as an 'other', so he/she has the chance to get in contact with their own other. Usually not being part of the patient's past helps in recognizing us as different from the patient's fantasies. Nazi-time, however, is a common history for both, either personally or as one belonging to a certain generation. If we are not conscious about the destructive effects of that history in our souls, we are not capable of offering ourselves as the 'good enough other'. Then, defences come up and mute silence is the consequence.

Talking to Neo-Nazis is difficult as well, possibly more so than when talking to our patients. Neo-Nazis refuse to see and try to understand the destructive parts of their own souls, and they attack and try to destroy the other. So, our fear of them has a double meaning; we fear by meeting with them that we will get in touch with ourselves and we fear to be destroyed by their attacks on the other – that we are not able to offer ourselves as the 'good enough other'.

More than in any other connection, a conscious knowledge about ourselves seems to be important. To achieve this knowledge and then to be able to offer oneself as a good enough other, presumes a meeting with oneself and, that is, what the conferences provide – these opportunities.

The conferences facilitate the organizing of time, room, safe boundaries and a 'good enough other', giving us the chance for a meeting with ourselves. Integration of destructive fantasies and impulses is the only safe way to stop destructive action, but our historical background it seems nearly impossible.

To conclude, I will use a quotation by Ernesto Che Guevara: *'Let us be realistic, let us try the impossible.'* (Eva Maria Staudinger).

***

"The conference members from Berlin tried to do something 'useful' for our present day German society, based on what we got out of the conference. We wanted to warn society – whoever this is – of antisemitic-foreigner's hate tendencies, in explaining its psychodynamics in form of critical papers of each of us in the group in response to a recent right wing pamphlet. We discovered our main anxieties in fighting 'them' in very concrete fears about our property and families. 'These people' are dangerous. What we found out is that *we* could very easily turn into 'these people' when we are scared too much from anxieties from within and real outside dangers which may combine in an vicious circle. When we read aloud our inner transference transcription of this right wing antisemitic xenophobic pamphlet it took our breath, we hardly could continue. That was an expression of our countertransference reaction" (Thomas Erdmann).

***

In addition to the primary aim of the Conference, other issues came up and became the focus of unexpected attention and work. Nazareth I brought together for the first time the two German psychoanalytic societies (the DPG and the DPV). The organizing body invited both societies as they each answered to the criteria for membership. It was only during the conference that it became clear that this was an unusual and even historical encounter, and that apparently it was the presence of the Israelis that was necessary for it to occur. This first encounter gave rise to a working conference in Germany between the two societies that took place in 1996, the Seeon Conference.

***

"The fact that, almost incidentally, the subject of the history of the DPV and DPG also led to further alleviation of tension between the members of the two societies has something to do with the Israeli colleagues' interest in this history. They want to know why we have two societies. By telling them about it, we develop several versions together and finally come to speak about the 'prehistory', the time prior to the split: Eitingon, Jewish psychoanalyst and chairman of the first analytic institute in Germany, was driven out by the non-Jewish German colleagues and went to Israel. Perhaps, as one of the fantasies in the group has it, we were also coming together in Israel to see that he and his great-grandchildren, who are now living and working there, have survived" (Ursula Kreuzer-Haustein).

***

For some the outcome was less than expected.

"I feel the need to repeat that beyond making our mutual acquaintance and demonstrating that the Germans and Israelis can talk to each other in a friendly and civilized way, not much more seemed to me to have occurred at this first meeting (Naz I). I do not know whether a different form of gathering could have achieved more and created more insight and have uncovered each one's method of denial.

It is of course possible that I who for years been acquainted with many Germans am rushing ahead here and am expecting more than an initial acquaintanceship and that this was already a necessary and useful first step for most of the participants. Anyway I believe that a follow up could indeed lead to a greater human openness towards each other, reach a richer self discovery of the roots of one's mourning, prejudice, hate and guilt. Such an aim is most desirable …

Psychoanalytic self-observation and psychoanalytical observation of others had convinced me, that only in actual contacts with persons from the 'other side' could an amelioration come about of the intrapsychic, interpersonal and even inter-territorial restrictions with which the perpetrators of the Nazi-crimes as well as their surviving victims have lived and which, beyond them, were carried further into the lives of their offspring. I fear that those who actually lived through the Nazi-period and its horrors will never be fully enabled to entirely work through the ego-impairments caused by their traumatization during the Nazi-terror. What can at best be achieved in their case is a diminution of their vulnerabilities created by these events. Unconscious and conscious guilt feelings and feelings of shame and deep feelings of grief are likely to stay with them as persistent shadows throughout their lives. This will be true, equally for the perpetrators of the Nazi-crime as well as for the surviving victims. But there is at least some hope that the offspring – touched only tangentially by the horror of these crimes, and affected by the holocaust either through 'delegation' or by other personal factors – cab obtain some relief from the above enumerated ego restrictions through group-therapeutic measures. This is indeed what is to be achieved by means of the Nazareth-Meetings. In fact, those persons from both sides, who attend them stem largely from the second or third post-holocaust generation. I do think that a degree of success has up to now been achieved in these meetings. When, in the following, a critical analysis will be attempted, it is expressed only with the aim of facilitating further progress and a deepening of the process.

With the thought in mind that the goal of our Meeting 'Germans and Israelis – The Past in the Present' had been to find ways to revise our mutual basic 'FIEND' fantasies I believe that a combination of affectively expressive, cognitively enriching and transferentially uncovering approaches must be used. Such an experience may enable the participant individual to continue, on his/her own, the work of self-exploration of the thoughts and feelings aroused in him/her during the encounter with the colleagues of the other national group" (Martin Wangh).

***

"For many of us, at a personal level, this event was extremely helpful and enriching in working through some of the feelings that have lived inside us for so many years. Nevertheless, in view of some of the events that have been happening in Germany these last few years, I couldn't avoid to think that in spite of its importance for us, *this experience is a drop in the sea and that reality is not necessarily what happened in Nazareth*" (Irene Melnick).

***

"We have to be careful in approaching the topic of incompetence. I dread to see the Germans marching again, even though the tune may not be the same: politics is a good guise. Personally, I feel easier as a German and with Germans, humbled through recognition of some the German truths.

The question of disablement is an important phenomenon that I have known from experience. The Kleinian contribution to exploring the ego destructive superego may be of some use here. But I would need to think a lot more about this before I could contribute to this" (Hella Ehlers).

***

"A few German participants concur in their description that they had overcome some of the numbing guilt feelings and scruples, so that they were now able to listen to the accounts related by individual Israelis about the horrors of the Holocaust more freely and were more interested in hearing them. The painful acceptance of historical guilt had grown; unproductive diffuse entanglements in guilt had become milder. Corresponding to this, a few Israelis had the impression that now we really wanted to hear something from them, about their personal story (of suffering). It comes to an interested, lively exchange about one's own fathers and mothers, 'the Jewish-ness' and 'the German-ness', about political assessments of the current right-wing radicalism and anti-Semitism in Germany and what is being done about it there. An Israeli woman whose mother survived the concentration camp tells about how much more easily her little daughter can talk with grandmother about the traces of the concentration camp experience than she herself can. As a little girl, she says, she had only inquired very late what the number tattooed on her mother's arm meant. For many years, she had protected herself against the shock of finding out that the tattoo was a concentration camp number by telling herself that all mothers had a number like that" (Ursula Kreuzer-Haustein).

***

"Tears are Better than Blood and Words are Better than Tears"

"The GIC for me is one way to not become petrified like Lot's wife by looking back. I mean this quite physically: not to fall into pieces, not to become ashes, but alternatively laughing and leaning on the graveyards where I have to live, there is no other place. I hope next time I will not be bleeding so much. My body seems to be the containment for what is at the time unbearable.
Tears are better than blood and words are better than tears; it is a permanent struggle to get through the words" (Irmgard Salzman).

***

"It is pain, their pain, not hate, pain which they suffer from in our true meaningful interactional process. How grateful I am for this experience. Somebody in the last plenary asked if the check of confidential mutual trust regained, would be covered (it was about a dream). I am freed to feel terribly sorry and ashamed. The process has the quality of coming to life again by this feeling sorry reached over my Jewish friend's pain being torn between his wish to follow my invitation to my Berlin home and his mother's warning: 'Don't, they killed your grandparents.'
Of course it was an unbearable moment when we stood in the Holocaust-Tower of the Jewish Museum in Berlin, silent, together" (Thomas Erdmann).

***

"May be, some people asked you in advance to tell about it afterwards. Suddenly, nobody wants to know. Perhaps you, too, don't want to reveal your inner feelings. If you are lucky, you have some friends, but don't be disappointed if not.
Participating in such a conference is like a walk in the mountains: there are beautiful moments and dangerous parts and afterwards everybody tells another story, what impressed him or her most. And sometimes you are astonished, how deep precipices are trivialized afterwards" (Eva Mack).

***

"What I have written is, of course, far from complete with view to my experiences during and after the conference. Rather, it encloses those ideas which I have, with the support of several Israeli and German colleagues, been able to work on, up to now. And this work continues. My perception of what happens in our country with view to our past has been sharpened, and I have begun to detect the defence against guilt and shame even in my (and others') upright criticism of signs of present antisemitism in our country – it is such a relief for me/us to detect it in others! It is so difficult to face my/our own destructiveness" (Veronika Grueneisen).

***

"I remember the next session vaguely; I wasn't really listening. I have no idea what led me, at some point, to listen for their names and to connect their names with their faces. First it happened and only afterwards did I notice that it was happening. I played with the names, some of them foreign and cold – Rolf, Gertrude, Carl, Werner, Ziegfried, Thomas – and some softer – Michael, Gisela, Veronika, Christoph, Uschi. I know it won't seem strange if I say that gradually, to my total surprise, they began to seem human" (Yoram Hazan).

***

IV.7   To be staff in these Conferences

Being staff in these Conferences is different from being staff in a "usual" Group Relations conference. People joined the staff group with a personal motivation and a personal history that is relevant to the theme. There is a higher level of involvement. It is not uncommon to have moments during a conference in which it is hard for a staff member to contain the emotions, being moved to tears is not rare, and so are dreams or nightmares.

The staff group has its own dynamic that is interrelated with the dynamic of the conference as a whole: it is reflected in it and reflective of it. An example might illustrate the dynamic and its intensity. Staff starts to work on their own dynamics in preparation for the conference a day or two before the conference. On the pre-conference staff meeting of the first Nazareth as we were talking about ourselves and our motivations, I said that Israelis have this automatic reaction when meeting Germans, of assessing the age of the person ("How old was he during the war") and then wondering what did that person or his parents do during the war. Silence fell in the group and one of the German staff member started to tell what his father did during the war, then another German staff did the same. The third German staff member became very upset and declared that she is not willing to be persecuted by this question! It was the end of the encounter at that moment, but the question, the answers and the non-answers were to loom over the conference all along.

***

Identity

"Being born in Frankfurt/M in 1937, my family – parents, older sister and I – lived through the terrible events and persecution that culminated in Kristallnacht and our escape from Germany, to what was to become Israel, in December 1938. I was raised in a home atmosphere through which I experienced, on an almost daily basis, the pain of having been torn, expelled and vomited as unwanted by a culture and language that was nonetheless an unchanging part of my parents' identity, and through them, of my own. In my formative years, I was never physically a 'Jew in Germany', yet most of the time very much a 'German Jew'. I came back to Germany for the first time on my 40th birthday, and numerous times since then. Each and every time I have had the uncanny experience of being 'back home', and at the same time – of being a total stranger and outsider, very much wanted or barely tolerated, as the case may be.

My countertransferential involvement is difficult and complicated. In an uncanny and turbulent way, this conference mobilizes the foundations of personal identity. The conference is actually about feelings and fantasies about *three* components: 'German-ness', 'Israeli-ness' and 'Jewish-ness'. This is my own interpretation of the statement in the brochure, which regards these as *two*, not three components. I personally have been fashioned by all three. I experienced these different parts of my own history, development and makeup as pulling me in different directions, dictating and demanding very different responses and actions. I could feel myself a Diaspora Jew, and an Israeli, yet at the same time in touch with a German part in me. This German part comes with my mother's milk and tongue. By taking part in these conferences, and by speaking about it, I am also engaged in a personal quest. It is the quest to harbor these internal parts without being torn apart by them, but also without denying them. The discovery of such personal links between internally feuding part-objects is what these conferences help make possible. In the final analysis, this is what they are all about" (H. Shmuel Erlich).

***

"I grew up in East and West Berlin, and my young days were shaped by the awareness of the consequences of Hitler's war, ruins all over a divided city. Both my parents came from conservative families, but joined the 'Confessional Church' which was strongly against Hitler, antisemitism and war. Nevertheless, it was beyond question that my father should serve in the Wehrmacht. Very early, my parents knew about concentration camps and the Holocaust. My mother saw to it that we knew what had happened. As an adolescent, I despised people who would insist on saying they hadn't known about what had happened. I had to come to Nazareth to understand that some possible questions I never asked, in my family, and that in –spite of all my knowledge I had not wanted to know what my father went through, as a soldier in the Wehrmacht. It had been so safe to believe that involvment in what the Nazis had done had nothing to do with me. The Nazareth I – experience as a member helped me to see more and begin to face my own destructiveness and my defence against it.

I worked in further training for people working in adult education, for many years. When I became aware of a need for further training, I chose psychoanalysis. I work as an analyst and training analyst of the German Psychoanalytic Society. Psychoanalysis has helped me to face ambivalence and the power involved in leadership roles, to develop my way of working with groups and unconscious processes relevant to the issues of a given seminar. I extended this learning through the Tavistock Institute's Programme for

Advanced Organisational Consultation, reconceptualised a programme for people in leadership roles in social organisations which incorporated some of group relations tradition and now work additionally as an organisational consultant.

The main feature of my experience as staff member in the conference in Bad Segeberg, 2000, was the feeling of not being 'on safe grounds', right from the pre-conference period throughout the conference itself up to the time after. This feeling immediately recurred when I was asked to write a contribution for publication, with view to my staff role experience. I understand this feeling as addressing the anxiety to encounter the 'past in the present', i.e. what I consider to be my competence might turn into something destructive.

In my role as German administrator in the conference in Bad Segeberg, I felt both chosen and unwanted, needed and put down in my capacity to contribute, in role. During the conference itself, I often felt flooded by feelings of fragility and incompetence. At the same time, I remember the enormous difference between the way I experienced myself and the way I was experienced by my colleagues. Relating to one of Eric Miller's hypotheses during the conference, I attribute my feeling fragile and a failure, paranoid and almost loosing my sense of identity, at times, to a defence against the anxiety that my competence and strength might, in fact, turn out to be destructive in working with my Israeli colleagues, I might be (come) a poisoning 'normal Nazi mother'.

Maybe, my experience of not feeling 'on safe grounds' was also related to representing, as I understand it, 'the second generation' on the staff: All other colleagues had been staff members, in the first conference. Both Israeli and German staff members had worked hard, for many years, to create this conference and make it happen, whereas I had been a member in the first conference, in Nazareth.

I understand that I came to be on the staff not because of my involvement in the dialogue between Israeli and German analysts. Instead, I was asked in, 'chosen' for my professional Group Relations competence and my membership in the German Psychoanalytic Society. However, initially, I was not fully authorised. A certain reproachfulness over against my 'first generation' colleagues, before and in the beginning of the conference, my feelings of fragility and incompetence during the conference may have mirrored some of the emotions of the German post war analysts over against their psychoanalytic (fore-) fathers who had been involved in expelling their Jewish colleagues from Nazi Germany. Accusing them allowed me to insist on not being guilty in their way – as I and many of my generation had done with our parents. Accusing them expressed, maybe, also the disappointment over the wish to identify with and idealise – then: psychoanalysis; now: the German-Israeli dialogue as represented in the conference" (Veronika Grueneisen).

***

"In one of the Plenaries in Bad-Segeberg, I referred to myself as being 'milked with tears'. I am an immediate post-war child, born in Palestine in 1944 to parents of Polish origin that came to Palestine as young pioneers and Zionist idealists, at the late 1920's.

While my entire father's family followed him to Palestine, and where saved, all my mother's family refused her insistent pleas for them to come on religious rounds: the Messiah has not arrived yet, so it is a sin to return to our Promised Land. They were all exterminated by the Nazis in Poland, none of them survived.

In the autumn of 1944 the news of what went in Europe started to filter to Palestine. My mother received bits and pieces of the terrible news, constructed the family story and fell into a deep depression, from which she never fully recovered. She lived passed my 50th birthday had a full and productive life, mainly devoted to the underprivileged.

I was breast-fed by the joy of her having me mixed with tears of her sorrow and desperation. I had the unconscious role of making up for her what she lost. I had to 'milk' her with hope and a sense of life.

Any mention of her lost father, brothers, sisters and their children would cause her such pain that I ended by just knowing their names. I know their names mainly because she put all their names on her tomb, while she prepared it for herself. Evidently none of them has a tomb. I know just their names, nothing else: not were they lived, what they did, what kind of people they were. How old each of them was. I am left with some pictures and 12 names.

The Eichmann trial echoed through my adolescence. I read all the available books on the Shoa. The Demianiuk trial accompanied me to my first Leicester Group Relation Conference.

Becoming a Psychoanalyst was a natural step. Doing the German-Israeli work was less so. It came out of professional meetings with Germans in which I realized aside from my ambivalence the need to be 'used' by the German colleagues to work through their position, and my need to 'use' them to have the courage to go beyond the wordless pain" (Mira Erlich-Ginor).

***

"I would like to report on the most acute experience that I myself had with myself during the three conferences. It is one of the results of the conference that I can report it now, which I was not yet able to do in Bad Segeberg.
  The staff members were sitting together in the restaurant on the evening that was free during the conference. We knew that we had really worked hard the past few days and felt that we had done good work. I was sitting at the end of a long table, across from me Jona Rosenfeld, originally from Hamburg, next to him Karin Lüders, to my right Rafael Moses, originally from Berlin, one of the fathers of these conferences, a friend whom I owe an entire development. He was eating roast venison with cranberries, and the roast seemed a bit tough. We were joking around. I said to him: 'You have to eat the cranberries with the meat. Otherwise it will taste too much like Buchenwald (beechwood).' I said Buchenwald. I turned cold as ice when I heard what I'd said and I looked into an abyss. Karin tried to keep me from falling.
  Every human being can imagine the dimensions of this parapraxis. I dared not to publish it while at the conference. I'm sorry for what I said, I can't begin to say how sorry I am. But the main thing is: I am getting to know myself from the acutely revealing experience. It is an effect of the conference. In my opinion, it belongs to the anti-Semitism *after* the Holocaust, which I am even more afraid of than that which made the Holocaust. The parapraxis consists of the projection of a German melancholy after the Holocaust, combined with a form of revenge against the victims, against a friend, for my sense of having a part in it and a responsibility, which is growing deeper and which I am also able to feel much more strongly in a collective sense, and don't want to keep feeling over and over again" (Hermann Beland).

***

IV.8 No Way and no Reason to Sum Up

There is no way and no reason to sum up or conclude this collage. It is open ended and only one version of the total experience. But it must come to an end, and for that end I chose two contributions having to do with the question of identity in relation to the German Israeli Conferences.

***

Identity was indeed an essential and central theme in this conference. The "ordinary Nazi mother" is an image of a poisonous breast, exuding venom and death, of which the child is a victim. It was impressive to see the crucial significance of food in the relationship with parents and culture. A German man exclaimed in angry disbelief, "My relationship with my mother was all around 'fresh potatoes!'" Food, smell and touch are some of the elements out of which the earliest sense of self and identity, of psychosomatic existence and being rooted in one's cultural soil, are constructed. But identity, the lifelong sense of our own self and "me-ness", is also defined by the image of the other, the "not-me", which it includes and uses. The German identity was burdened with shame and guilt, and was experienced as handicapped and incapacitating. In the German identity, the Jew is an 'Other' who occupies a special place. He or she is ambivalently regarded as possessing aliveness and wisdom, making him an object of both desire and envious attack. Within the German identity, there seems to be embedded an elemental Jewish component as an idealized/envied/hated other.

In the Israeli/Jewish identity, different issues were apparent. The part of the other is not necessarily German. The other, for the Israelis, can take on many different faces – European, Arab or the catchall non-Jewish/Gentile. It is indeed part of Jewish identity that *anyone* may take the role of the stranger and persecutor.

These issues around identity become even more painful when identity is undergoing change. The changed image of the other causes a shift in the perception of oneself. If the other is an invaluable determinant of one's own identity, then, as the image of the other undergoes change, it causes the personal and collective group identity to change with it. This change is experienced as a serious threat on all psychic levels: it destabilizes one's sense of the world as an organized, coherent, meaningful place. It undermines the clarity of delineation of good and bad objects, upsetting habitual patterns of projection and creating havoc with ambivalent splits of love and hate. It upsets the primitive schizo-paranoid order, but does not allow progressive movement to a depressive integration. Worst of all, however, it undermines one's ties and roots in psychic and social reality. The changed perception of the other militates against the view of the world that was part of the emotional ties with one's parents and family. It is an assault on the family ego (Klein & Erlich 1976).

In the System Event, such threats to identity clearly emerged as a result of Germans and Israelis coming in close contact. Because the conference has shaken deeply established identity patterns, by changing one's view of oneself and the other, it produced the disarray, tension and upset described. It is difficult to give up familiar roles, such as the role of perpetrator for the Germans, and that of victim for the Israelis. The overriding danger blocking change is the fear of *betrayal* – of parents, relatives and culture – and the associated shame and guilt (H. Shmuel Erlich).

***

"I am not always sure that I am not betraying the memory of the past. On the other hand, there is something in the attempt that fascinates me. It is like traveling somewhere that no one has been before us, with the only possible partners to be with there. We did not choose the other, he was there, and thus we became partners. Pictures of our parents and those of our partners are always in the background. I have no words for the end; after all, we are just beginning" (Yoram Hazan).

IV.9 List of Contributors

Staff
Beland Hermann
Erlich H. Shmuel
Erlich-Ginor Mira
Miller Eric

Israeli
Gotesfeld Johana
Hazan Yoram
Cohen Daniela
Litvin Ilana & Mendelson Itzhak
Melnick Irene
Friedman Robi
Wangh Martin
Weisman-Zahor Pnina

German
Bierman Christoph
Dettbarn Irmgard
Ehlers Hella
Erdmann Thomas
Grueneisen Veronika
Kreuzer-Haustein Ursula
Mack Eva
Matzner-Eicke Jutta
Nedelmann Carl
Pollmann Armin
Salzman Irmgard
Staudinger Eva-Maria
Schulte-Herbrüggen Odo
Strauss Vivianne
Wittmann Thea
Zitzelsberger-Schlez Angelika

V Central and Emergent Themes

H. Shmuel Erlich

V.1 Holocaust-Related Identity Components of Germans and Israelis

When we think about the post-Holocaust encounter of Israeli Jews and Germans, the themes that readily come to mind are likely to be emotionally colored and weighted. We can anticipate feelings of hatred, murderousness and vengeance on one side, and fear of retaliation, guilt and yearning for atonement and forgiveness on the other. Further psychological contents and forces may easily be introduced: defensive withdrawal, avoidance and denial, contempt for weakness and vulnerability, or moral superiority.

Naturally, such feelings and emotional dynamics were abundant in the conferences. And yet, expectable as they were, it is doubtful whether the emergence and expression of these feelings and dynamics constituted the most instructive and valuable of the conference's revelations. When we reflect upon the meaning and eventual yield of the conferences, it seems that the most poignant and salient points have less to do with emotional contents, and much more with certain enduring patterns which may best be described as *identity issues*.

While identity has become a household term, it is still difficult to define psychologically and even more so psychoanalytically. Yet this difficulty has to do with what actually makes it such a valuable concept. Identity has a double-faced nature: it is rooted in *both* the significant realms in which life transpires. On one hand, it is outwardly directed towards the social and cultural milieus which define and contextualize our existence as social beings. But on the other hand, it is as much inner-directed and taps the deeply personal function of maintaining one's sense of sameness and being oneself over time and against shifting external backgrounds. The dilemma is thus more a dilemma of definition and understanding than a real problem. In actuality, of course, our Janus-faced identity is capable of performing both functions, and moreover – typically and where no untoward difficulties beset it – of integrating both dimensions quite smoothly. This integration is what enables us to function with a clear sense of who we are, where and whether we belong as a part of the group we are in, and the extent to which we truly are ourselves, both before and after.

Identity was indeed an essential and central theme in these conferences. It was impressive, for instance, to see the crucial significance of food in the relationship with parents and culture. In Bad Segeberg, many Israelis experienced strange sensations of early familiarity and primary identity with the smell and character of the food which they recognized as typical of their parental home and kitchen. In a different vein, a German man exclaimed in angry disbelief, "My relationship with my mother was all around 'fresh potatoes'!" Food, smell and touch are some of the elements out of which the earliest sense of self and identity, of psychosomatic existence and of being rooted in one's cultural soil are constructed. The "ordinary Nazi mother" is another image of a poisonous breast, exuding venom and death, of which the child is a victim.

But identity, the lifelong sense of our own self and "me-ness", is also defined by the image of the other, the "not-me", which it includes and makes use of. The German identity was burdened with shame and guilt, and was experienced as handicapped and incapacitating. In the German identity, the Jew is an 'Other' who occupies a special place. He or she is ambivalently regarded as possessing aliveness and wisdom, making him an object of both desire and envious attack. Within the German identity, there seems to be embedded an elemental Jewish component as an idealized/envied/hated Other.

Yet these wishes and fantasies are only the presenting difficulties. As conference dynamics unfold, these issues are replaced by increasingly deeper concerns, malaise and pain. One of the striking findings about the Germans is their ubiquitous experience of growing up in families in which they experienced themselves – in a great variety of ways – as the victims of overall decent and yet obtuse parents, who cared for them physically but were often unaware of them emotionally. This rupture and its uncanny consequence – being materially looked after with nothing to complain about on one level, yet feeling totally forsaken and neglected on another (as in the "fresh potatoes" comment) – makes for a maddening dilemma and split in one's self-image and ego ideal, and at the same time, it severely hampers the ego's capacity for fully and emotionally relating to its objects. For the most part this feeling was directed at the mothers, as reflected in the emblematic expression by a German member: "I was raised by an ordinary Nazi mother." Indeed, some of the stories reported by German members about their mothers were devastating for the dearth of emotional contact they reflected, coupled with overwhelming efforts to make everything appear smooth, normal and fully appropriate. It was often the feeling of the non-Germans, particularly of the Jews, that these German members were the child victims of severe emotional abuse.

This emotional deprivation repeated itself over different conferences and changing memberships. It seems to reveal a fundamental aspect of parent-child relationships in German families of the War time and following decades. One can only wonder and speculate about the essential truth revealed here about the finer and darker parts of the early object relations experienced by German infants and children, and the possible effects of this on German society and history. Certainly this would represent a rather far reaching conclusion. But at the immediate level, one could observe several characteristic traits of German members that would seem directly related to this severe difficulty.

One such manifestation is the way in which aggression is handled and expressed. Two essential formations stand out in this connection, typified to a greater or lesser extent by different personalities: One formation may be characterized as a reaction formation in which the person becomes "good" to such an extent that s/he is completely unable to experience negative feelings, is always understanding, sympathetic, helpful, and ready to accede to the other's point of view. This type of person is experienced as pleasant, cultured, perhaps cerebral, and always very much self-contained. Yet it is very difficult to enter into full or open relatedness with him or her, and conversation seems to trail off and die for lack of "oxygen". The other type is more troublesome: It is a person who is superficially pleasant, but is not at all well defended against his own aggression. This person is full of aggressive and perverse fantasies which s/he experiences consciously, yet has no inkling about their source or object and is deeply troubled by them. This person is prone to express his or her aggressive feelings and raging fantasies quite openly, usually in an emotionally flat manner, and is quite surprised when others respond with fear, shock and withdrawal. It is not easily understood that this "frank" and "open" expression of aggressive fantasies is actually not what it purports to be, but a cry for help and an expression of utter loneliness and pain that is often out of awareness.

What I have described so far are individual, interpersonal ways of coping with the experience of emotional distance coupled with correct external care and handling. There are other ramifications of these observations that become evident only at the group level. The German group often seemed to lose its bearings among several possible modes of action and reaction. Its preferred way was to be imprisoned by fear of open aggression – of confrontation, struggle and strife – and to prefer a course of endless "civilized" discussion and debate, conducted in the most orderly and democratic way, but in effect becoming completely paralyzed and unable to act in a timely fashion, thus becoming gradually irrelevant. A different but related manifestation was to become extremely efficient and task oriented in a way that might be oblivious of or cruelly disregard the feelings and concerns of others.

Another expression of this difficulty was the feeling of shame the German members seemed to struggle with. This was evident especially in large group settings, where Germans often felt tongue tied, shy, and ashamed of their poor command of English (the language used in such multi-national settings). Although most non-Germans were just as inarticulate, they seemed to be much less hampered by this disadvantage. In effect, the often obviously superior capacities of the Germans for thinking and reflecting were not at all realized by them, and they would habitually see themselves as stupid, imperceptive and inferior to the Israelis and Jews. Clearly they were hampered by shame and guilt.

All of these emotions and feelings bear directly on the issue of identity. Several aspects are relevant to this issue: psychoanalytic, national, legal, and personal. The conferences underscore the great extent to which all of these are intertwined and interconnected. In the first place, it seems that the German *psychoanalytic* identity, as it came through in these conferences, tends to be uneasy and conflicted, perhaps because it is burdened by the need to identify with Freud – a Jewish father figure – and the historical patricidal and fratricidal "killing off" of Jewish colleagues during the Nazi regime. These are painful facts that are difficult to deny and may forever plague the German psychoanalytic conscience. Furthermore, the great pain and isolation carried by German analysts from their childhood, described above, might well play a role in their self-selection to become psychoanalysts. It is undeniable that what brings psychoanalysts to their profession always includes a formidable component of personal history, the experience of pain and conflict, and the wish for reparation, perhaps even for redemption. Every culture has its own patterns of object relations that affect parenting and early life experience in specific ways – perhaps this should be more carefully studied and elaborated. The experience of these conferences, however, points to a very serious conflict and possible deficit in the early object relations that affect German children, and thus eventually German psychoanalysts. All these factors are part of the foundation of the German psychoanalytic identity, and give rise to self-searching, discomfort and unease, and consequently to attempts to counteract these by an overemphasis on upstanding "professionalism". Yet this "professionalism" may recapitulate deep seated feelings of distance and the pain of not being fully understood and related to.

The personal, legal and nationalistic aspects of these identity dilemmas are made even more painfully obvious through the presence of German-Jewish psychoanalysts – Jewish colleagues who live and work in Germany. Their identities are understandably extremely conflicted and burdened with the difficulty of finding their own rightful and comfortable place. Their specific issues serve to underscore the more general problem of the German analysts who, while in numerous ways a successful majority, tend at times to experience themselves as a beleaguered and unsafe minority.

One of the most striking ways this last point manifested itself in the conferences is through the envy that the Germans openly expressed toward the Israeli-Jewish members. Although the Germans were clearly and in many ways the major group, they perceived the Israelis as the strong ones, and readily idealized them as powerful, united and possessing a clear sense of group and individual identity. It seems that what the Germans envied the Israelis most for was their seeming vitality, and the way this seemed to cement and color their relationships, in stark contrast to the Germans' more removed and isolated social experience.

This also explains another emergent finding: the extent to which the Germans mourn the absence and disappearance of "their" Jews. It is as if the deeply rooted German ambivalence succeeded in getting rid of a beloved as well as hated object which is missed and longed for.

In the Israeli/Jewish identity, different issues were apparent. The part of the Other is not necessarily reserved for the Germans. For the Israelis, the Other can take on different faces – European, Arab, or the catchall non-Jewish/Gentile. It is indeed part of Jewish identity that *anyone* may take on the role of the stranger-enemy and persecutor. In the third conference, however, the 'Other' for the Israelis became the "non-Israeli" Diaspora Jew. Feared and resented, the anger of the group threatened to focus on and scapegoat him. To an extent, this had to do with the greater affinity of the Diaspora Jew to the Germans. In another respect, it represented the rejection of the Diaspora Jew who is experienced as the negative of and a threat to the newly won "Israeli" identity. This recapitulates modern Jewish and Zionist history: In the pre-state era of Zionist settlement, and later in the newly created State of Israel, there was a powerful rejection and negation of Diaspora Jews, both before and even more so after the Holocaust. This rejection manifested itself primarily and principally at the level of identity formation, where everything related to the Diaspora Jew had to be discarded and suppressed – religion, history, language, cultural roots and physical characteristics.

The Israelis presented themselves as self-assured, strong and fearless, but also as sympathetic and ready listeners. A peculiar mixture of brashness and sensitivity seemed to characterize them, at least at the start. With time and the development of conference dynamics, other, more recessive and suppressed features became evident, accompanied by chagrin and pain. The self-assurance seemed to hide confusion and ignorance about the Other from whom they have been separated and protected by a secluded and beleaguered life.

The Holocaust and its aftermath are an important part of Israeli identity, albeit as a negative identity. In this sense, the ambivalence experienced and expressed towards the Diaspora Jewish identity is clearly a reaction – of denial and displacement – towards the Diaspora component that is built into the new Israeli identity. Another important aspect of this is the constant tension experienced between the diametrically opposed victim posture and that of hero and even super-hero. A byproduct of this tension is the ready relapse into a paranoid stance, in which one feels attacked and victimized by the world merely for being Israeli.

The most striking and troublesome finding was the emergence of power struggles within the Israeli group, which soon took on the character of what some of them described as a "Fascist" takeover. There seemed to be a very thin line separating strength and powerfulness from directly expressed aggression and an open bid for dominating the group in the face of divergence and disagreement. One may discern a subtle shift in the identity of the Israelis from the first conference (in Nazareth), in which they experienced themselves as a persecuted minority, to the third conference (in Bad Segeberg) in which this in-group aggression broke out. Perhaps these phenomena were fueled and set in motion in each case by the specific venue – the beleaguered identity in Israel changing into the "Fascist" one in Germany, where the Israelis felt more threatened and reverted to identification with the aggressor.

For both Germans and Israelis, these difficult identity issues become even more painful when identity undergoes change. The changed image of the other sets in motion a corresponding shift in the perception of oneself. If the other is an invaluable determinant of one's own identity, then, as the image of the other undergoes change, it causes the personal and collective group identity to change with it. This change is experienced as a serious threat on all psychic levels: it destabilizes one's sense of the world as an organized, coherent and predictable place. It undermines the clear delineation of good and bad objects, upsetting habitual patterns of projection and creating havoc with ambivalent splits of love and hate. It upsets the primitive schizo-paranoid order, yet is incapable of making the progressive movement to a depressive integration. Worst of all, however, it undermines one's ties and roots in psychic and social reality. The changed perception of the other militates against the view of the world that was part of the emotional ties with one's parents and family. It is an assault on the family ego (Klein/Erlich 1976).

In the System Event, such threats to identity clearly emerged as a result of Germans and Israelis coming into close contact with each other. Because the conference had shaken deeply established identity patterns by changing one's view of oneself and the other, it produced the disarray, tension and upset experienced by the participants. It is difficult to give up familiar roles, such as the role of perpetrator for the Germans and that of victim for the Israelis. One sensed danger is the shifting and uncertain nature of the new social order. Yet another danger blocking change is the fear of *betrayal* – of parents, relatives and culture – and the associated shame and guilt. It is as if one's closest allies would never understand the change one has undergone, would feel let down and betrayed, and will withdraw their love and support. Identity shifts and changes are thus accompanied not only by feelings of shame and guilt, but by the troubling fear of loosing one's secure footing in the world, of becoming an outcast and being exposed to rebuff and loneliness. This and similar fantasies are the major obstacle to transforming one's identity.

V.2 Special Trauma and Special Relationships

Trauma serves as a key concept in psychodynamic approaches. The deleterious effects of trauma are typically understood in quantitative and dynamic terms: overwhelming of normal capacities for processing and channeling an injurious onslaught; and subsequent collapse of the usual adaptive measures. To what extent are these explanations applicable to the traumata of the Holocaust? Is it possible – some would even ask if it is permissible – to conceive of the Holocaust and its aftermath in terms of trauma? Where and when does our usual understanding of trauma have to make way for another kind of understanding?

A great deal has been written about such questions, in the professional as well as in popular literature and fiction. It is not our intention to review this vast literature or to add to it. Yet these dilemmas that are inextricably part of the Holocaust are at the root of the conferences described in this volume and thus cannot be avoided. It is not so much the question of how some were able to survive and others not, but of the scar left by the Holocaust on ever widening circles of people whose lives were affected by it.

From the beginning, we thought that there was – more accurately, there is – a unique meaning to the trauma of the Holocaust. This unique trauma is related at its core to the special relationship that exists between Germans and Jews. This presumption is spelled out in the opening paragraph of the conference brochure:

> "There is a strange undercurrent of a 'special relationship' between Germans and [Israeli] Jews. This 'special relationship' is based on each people having been a partner, on different sides, to the terrible chain of events that took place between 1933 and 1945. The 'specialness' has to do with a fascination with this past history, an inability to mourn its disastrous effects and to deal with the implications of its continued shadowy presence. Germans and Israelis have adopted a variety of ways of dealing with this common past history ..."

The idea expressed in these lines is that the special bond joining Germans and Israelis/Jews is in their pairing as the inseparable participants on both sides of a destructive enactment of apocalyptic proportions – as victims and as perpetrators. There is no doubt about the validity and correctness of this view. Yet the work of the conferences produced an even more complex insight into the joining of these paired partners: there is a very deep current of emotional ambivalence, of love and hate, which pervades their historical relationship. There was ample evidence of German ambivalence: the Jews were idealized and exalted, were sorely missed and longed for, as if they were a cherished part that had been driven out and lost. For the Jews, murderous rage and vengefulness were more evident, but also deep envy and even a secret (unacceptable) need to identify with the Germans.

These ambivalent feelings are not easily identified or owned. The two groups – Germans and Israeli Jews – are quite distinct from one another in many respects. The very notion of a special relationship is met with great resistance on both sides. And yet, it helps explain and highlight many things, in both current political terms and in the persistent motivation to attend these conferences and make certain that this work continues despite many difficulties.

The idea of the special relationship is deeply intertwined with the question of the special trauma. Many reasons can be given for the special place occupied by the Holocaust in history and in present culture and society. From the point of view of the conferences, however, we may say that the specialness of the trauma of the Holocaust is directly related to this special relationship. The conscious and unconscious threads intertwining Jewish and German culture and history make the murderous wish for extermination horrendous beyond any proportion, and equally so the depth of betrayal and rejection suffered by the victims.

The Presence of the Other

The premise on which the conferences were based was that the work to be done – by the individual as well as the group – is enabled and made effective when done *in the actual presence of the other* who is the counterpart of one's burden. This assumption proved to be a most powerful ingredient as well as facilitator of the work.

Psychoanalytic work also demands the presence of the other. There is, however, a profound difference between this therapeutic presence and the one in the conference. In the psychoanalytic and psychotherapeutic setting, the other is in actuality an unrelated presence as regards one's own history and life story. It is this therapeutic presence – fully involved, yet not an actual participant in one's life – that engenders fantasy and the transference relatedness to this available other, thus providing the vehicle for interpretation, insight and change.

In the conference, on the other hand, the other is the actual counterpart to one's suffering and pain and one's burden of guilt and shame. In this sense, it is a related and participant other, not a removed or neutral one. In fact, there is no removed other in the conference, because everyone – even those not directly affected, or neither German nor Jewish – is in some way part of the legacy and impact of the Holocaust. In the attempt to deal with what happened in the aftermath of the Holocaust *within* both Germans and Jews we must also deal with what transpired *between* them. It makes all the difference in the world whether this work is performed exclusively at the level of internal fantasy, or in the presence of the other. It is especially telling if that other is actually a part of the psychic and historical reality in question.

Yet the conference methodology and way of working is neither confrontational nor conciliatory. It does not call for doing one's work *with* the other. Rather, it calls for doing both the individual and group work *in the presence* of the other, with the aim of being enabled to do one's own work by this presence.

This premise turns out to be extremely useful and important. It can be credited with the fact that the conference shuns the usual and more obvious goal of "working out the difficulties" with the other party in an interactive mode. Such aims are typically associated with themes of understanding, reconciliation and forgiveness, all of which are foreign to these conferences. Greater understanding of the other may of course be a product or byproduct of the work and certainly can and does happen; but it is not an expressed or implicit aim to be actively pursued. This makes the work much more powerful, free ranging and unpredictable, and hence also more effective, in whatever way such effectiveness can be estimated.

This stance may also militate against the resistance expressed by many on the Jewish/Israeli side: here the tendency is to view the conferences as openly or secretly striving to obtain reconciliation and atonement for the Germans, which many Israeli Jews are strongly and even vehemently opposed to. This view, while understandable, fails to comprehend and deal with the most important underpinning of the conference: that doing this work is as important for the Israelis/Jews in terms of their own Holocaust-related problems, regardless of whatever it means for others. This understanding, however, contributes little towards overcoming this specific resistance since it can only be gained by attending the conference and taking part in the work. It is incapable of overcoming such pre-conference resistance if it prevents people from coming.

V.3 Change and Transformation – the Burden of Betrayal

The primary task of the conference aims at exploration and learning through and from one's own experience and the experience of others. Specifically, it aims

> "To provide opportunities for participants to explore how feelings and fantasies about 'Germanness' and 'Israeliness/Jewishness' influence relations within and between the two groups in the conference."

Learning implies change and transformation: one is able to see things differently, to understand and become more aware of feelings, fantasies and dynamics of which one was unaware or which were opaque to him. Such altered capacities imply internal shifts and transformations. At the same time, they also imply that some resistance was overcome, weakened or removed. No new learning can take place without such a prior shift in resistance.

To enable the kind of exploration envisioned by the conference, this general resistance to learning must be overcome. This necessary process is enabled and set in motion by the conference methodology, its structure and design, which assist in reducing the general level of resistance ensconced in usual and familiar social defenses. But this is not the whole story. Psychoanalytic treatment teaches us that resistance may also serve as the royal road to the unconscious, pointing the way to whatever is in need of being covered, repressed and generally defended against. It is not surprising therefore that another major source of resistance was unraveled which could only be gleaned and encountered through the conference work. This particular resistance has to do with the issue of *betrayal*.

The overriding danger blocking change that emerged in these conferences is the fear of betrayal – of parents, relatives and culture – and the associated shame and guilt. The feeling of betrayal, as already mentioned, is connected with one's identity and primary identifications. In the first place, and especially on the part of the victims, the very act of coming to and attending the conference is felt to be a betrayal. The memory of dead relatives, of their suffering, persecution and humiliation is experienced as a command "never to forget, never to forgive". The very act of coming to the conference, of "sitting with Germans in the same room" as one colleague put it, is therefore an unthinkable betrayal of these memories and emotional ties. For many of the second and third generations of victims, whether directly affected or not, it falls under the same prohibition as stepping on German soil, using the German language, or listening to German music. This sense of betrayal acts as a powerful resistance against the very possibility of attending the conference.

But even for those who choose to come, the struggle with the danger of betrayal is present throughout the conference. It militates in the most fundamental ways against making direct contact with German participants and colleagues, as if the mere social acknowledgement of their presence and existence might constitute a betrayal. As faces, voices, foreign names and gestures become more familiar and recognizable, a deep split appears: one is aware of the other's humanity and existence, but at the same time one feels "committed" to preserve the perception of the other as a "perpetrator" who might have committed atrocities personally, or is closely associated with it as the son or daughter of perpetrators. This commitment is experienced in near religious terms, as an act of loyalty and preservation, a debt one owes to those of one's family who perished. It is religious in the sense that although rationally one may recognize the absurdity of the projections, one still feels that to give them up may undermine one's sense of identity and group affiliation.

Although this sense may be somewhat less pronounced and articulate for the Germans, it nonetheless is present and operative. The group affiliation here is through collective shame and guilt, but also through one's sense of what "Germanness" is all about and whether one can live with it, or for that matter without it.

The psychological mechanisms underlying this fear of betrayal are deeply rooted in familial and tribal affiliation and belonging. It is clear that to forgo and give up this sense of belonging is not only nearly impossible, but also extremely dangerous. The danger may have its primitive roots in demands for security and survival that are phylogenetically rooted. But further evolution and development have made this need no less basic and essential. The need to belong and be a part of a larger entity is still enormously powerful. One of the immediate consequences of this need is its obverse or negative side – the need to identify those who are *not* a part of one's family or tribe, and to label them as enemies, either potentially or actually. In the aftermath of the Holocaust it is clear where and how these lines of enmity would be drawn and how supportive and necessary they are for the maintenance of one's identity and social affiliation. In this sense the conference represents a dangerous threat to one's identity and affiliation which is experienced as betraying one's own group by crossing the lines into the "enemy camp". This is poignantly illustrated in the vignette related by the Israeli man whose mother warned him – actually enjoined him – against going with German friends, "Don't go with them! They killed your grandparents!"

It is difficult to say anything about how this powerful resistance in the form of the fear of betrayal is overcome, but at the same time it is clearly one of the achievements of the conferences for those who participated in them. Perhaps it has to do with the structure and method that enables the kind of experimentation that defuses the sense of betrayal. In the final analysis such experiments with "crossing the lines" may lead to a renewed and deeper commitment to one's own group, albeit from a newly gained position and perspective.

Outcome and Implications of the Conferences

What can be said about the outcome of the conferences? This is of course a very legitimate question, yet the answer cannot be straightforward. There are many reasons and explanations for this difficulty: Outcomes can only be measured and assessed against a primary task. The primary task of the conference is *exploration*, and more specifically – the exploration of fantasies, feelings and experiences. While this can be, and is a tangible and doable activity, its assessment is made difficult by the private and subjective nature of what is explored and experienced and its changing and transient nature. This is an inherent aspect of all here-and-now experiential events and processes, including psychoanalysis and psychotherapy – it is always extremely difficult, if not impossible, to isolate specific causal factors contributing to change or *the* most meaningful experiences. The difficulty of specifying causality does not indicate, however, that no change or development have taken place. While the conference is focused largely at the group level and on group events, it is the individual who experiences such change as may take place. In this sense, each participant can be said to have had his or her own conference, but this is not conducive to making generalizations about "the conference experience" or achievements.

Nevertheless, some general points can and need to be made. It is evident in the course of the conference how individuals are partaking of a highly charged experience that has much personal meaning for them. While this need not be universal or equal for everyone and is both subjective and private, it often finds expression in the public sphere as well. Perhaps the most important and meaningful indicator of how valuable the experience has been is the readiness to engage in this work in the first place, and beyond that – the willingness to engage in it repeatedly. A large proportion of the participants attended several conferences, suggesting that some valuable experiential learning had accrued and was valued by them. Lastly, the commitment of the staff as a group is another outstanding testimony to the high regard and value which this particular group attaches to the work.

Do the conferences have implications that reach beyond the boundaries of the specific event? Several themes come to mind, all of which have implications for further applications. One major implication concerns the place and meaning of the Holocaust: it is a huge gaping wound that refuses to scar over and be done with. Its shadow looms over so much of recent and current history and over more widely disparate groups than just Germans and Jews or Israelis. It cannot and will not be repressed or suppressed, efforts to do so notwithstanding. If we ever want to be able to lead lives that do not fall under this shadow, we must keep on dealing with the Holocaust and not shirk it.

Another implication has to do with the method: In these conferences we have discovered and developed a powerful methodology for dealing with inter-group enmities and historical strife and strain. Though certainly neither a mass remedy nor a panacea, this method may be applied effectively in similar situations and circumstances.

A further significant point that arises in conjunction with this special methodology has implications for currently prevalent ideas on conflict resolution. A much touted view holds that the most important, and perhaps sufficient, approach is to bring rivaling parties or enemy groups together under the same roof to help them "dialogue" with each other. This seems to be, among other reasons, an outgrowth of the psychotherapeutic culture that raises the banner of "Let's talk about it", as if the very act of talking can resolve difficulties. The experience gained in these conferences suggests that this view may well be colored by excess optimism and superficiality. Where dialogue can be established, the two sides are already ripe for joint work and have shifted in their perception of the other as an enemy (Erlich 1997, 2001). The approach taken in these conferences was rather different. Instead of aiming for dialogue, the task was for each group to work in the presence of the other group. The focus was thus not dialogic, but intra-group and inter-group directed, enabling projections about one's own and the other group to be explored and tested. This approach, as was stated above, proved much more powerful and avoided the typical pitfalls of denial of aggression and the production of a false and compliant emotional stance. Dialogue implies the prior recognition of the other's otherness and right to be what he is. This cannot be a direct goal; it can only emerge as the byproduct of a process which in itself need not be, and is not yet dialogic.

VI Post Conference Experience

H. Shmuel Erlich

VI.1 Presentations, Discussions, Their Impact and Contributions

The uniqueness of each and every Group Relations conference generally works against their public presentation. It is difficult, if not impossible, to render the experience, which is so subjective, private and at the same time multidimensional, shifting and complex, in the ordinary modes of oral or written accounts. Nor does it usually seem necessary to publicize it: individual participants take with them whatever they have learned or gleaned from the conference, often continuing their internal processing long after the event is finished. The conference director usually submits a report to the sponsoring organizations, which deals with some of the factual data – numbers, recruitment, financial issues, etc. – but contents itself with few very general remarks on the process, the main issues and the learning that took place.

Perhaps not surprisingly, this was not the case with these conferences. The idea of this volume, for example, came up fairly early, in recognition of its unique place and nature. At the same time, it is evident that the idea was difficult to carry out, as testified by the length of time it has taken to put together and produce this book. The idea of the book, however, came from the initiators and organizers of the conferences, who were also members of staff. It is therefore very noteworthy that independently of the initiative of the organizers, individual participants found it important to share their experiences with colleagues. This typically took the form of papers presented to several psychoanalytic institutes in Germany. These presentations faced the common difficulty of having to share with and explain to the audience information about the structure and design of the conference in order to make it intelligible. They focused mostly on the System Event as the most powerful experience within the conference. The difficulty these presenters faced was the same one as the authors of this volume: to share an experience that is highly personal and at the same time contingent upon certain formal features of setting and structure with an audience that has not experienced both. The effort was valiant, and the impact was significant: the conferences became a well-known entity within the German psychoanalytic community.

An important acknowledgement of the place and meaning of the conferences to German psychoanalysts came in the year 2000, when the German Psychoanalytic Association (DPV) celebrated its 50th anniversary. On this occasion a panel was devoted to Holocaust, Trauma, Collective Memory and Historical Awareness (Bohleber/Drews 2001) which included presentations of the Germans and Israelis Conferences by a German staff member (H. Beland) and an Israeli one (H. S. Erlich). This marked the first time this work was accorded national and international attention.

In the following years there were more presentations to various forums. In 2001 the work was presented at the Austen Riggs Center in Stockbridge, Massachusetts. In 2007 it was presented at IPTAR (Institute for Psychoanalytic Training and Research) in New York. The most significant presentation was undoubtedly at the International Psychoanalytic Congress in Berlin in 2007, where an entire panel was devoted to four presentations on the conferences by two Israelis and two Germans. In every one of these presentations there was a large, very much involved and eagerly receptive audience.

A further noteworthy outcome of the work took place at the 2007 Berlin IPA Congress and had an unusual impact. Because of the special significance of holding the Congress in Berlin, the Program Committee saw fit to ask us [the Editors] to conduct an experiential event in the Congress that would address the emotional issues stirred up by the Berlin venue. We designed and conducted an open and continuous Large Group event – *Being in Berlin* – that took place on each of the three days of the Congress and was attended by hundreds of people. It was a moving and significant event which many participants described as the heart and highlight of the Congress. This event would not have been possible without our experience in the conferences, and it represents a direct outcome and application of this work and the learning it made possible.

On what may be described the negative or obverse side, it must also be noted that in contrast to the importance given to this work in Germany and elsewhere, it was not accorded the same place in Israel. With one minor exception, none of the Israeli participants has written or presented this work to the Israel Psychoanalytic Society or to other forums. The one exception was a presentation included in a Day's Meeting of the Society that was devoted to the general topic of "The Society in Society", in which several applications and extensions of psychoanalytic work were presented. Another presentation took place as part of a lecture series in a large psychiatric hospital. This relative silence is consistent with the resistance to this work among Israelis described above. The same phenomenon was also evident in the *Being in Berlin* event, which the Israelis who attended the congress almost totally shunned. This negative phenomenon is especially noteworthy in view of the prominence given in Israel to the Holocaust and its aftermath on both public, formal and informal levels. Perhaps it is this very emphasis and the fact that the Holocaust is so much a part of Israeli life that makes it so difficult to engage in direct work with Germans, even when they are professional colleagues. At the same time, the response of those Israelis who attended the conferences was decidedly very positive, deeply involved and grateful.

VII Epilogue
H. Shmuel Erlich

VII.1 Where to Now?

The future of this project seems paradoxically both uncertain and yet quite secure. There is no doubt that the conference has established itself as a viable institution in the minds of German, Israeli and international psychoanalysts and psychotherapists. Interesting testimony to this viability is the assumption often heard that the conference takes place regularly every year, and if one does not attend on a particular date, it is always possible to "catch" the next one. The inclusion of the report on the conferences in the 50th anniversary celebration of the DPV and the International Psychoanalytical Association Congress also testifies to this. In this sense it will, and must, have a future.

Following Bad Segeberg, we opened a Website dedicated to the conference, with an Open Forum in which people could write in and communicate. It soon became a lively forum for discussion and exchange, again indicating both the interest and the need. The Forum was intended for conference participants and staff. After a period of about two years it was closed down for two reasons: Because of lack of adequate protection it fell pray to hostile and negative intruders on the internet. But it was also weighted down by the dominance of some writers to the detriment of others.

The uncertainty, however, lies in a different direction. For some, the third conference and its taking place on German soil represented the symbolic closing of a circle. The first two Nazareth Conferences enabled the Israeli participants to venture to come to Germany. For some participants, therefore, this in itself constituted sufficient change, as if by the act of coming to Germany the work was completed. For others, it implied that a change in the aim and focus of the conference was in order. It was suggested that the conference should expand its horizons beyond the German-Israeli-Jewish context; that it should be extended to other conflict areas and apply to them what has been learned and gained here. This is clearly a worthwhile goal, worthy of support and investment.

VII.2 Who Needs These Conferences?

The above described different viewpoints about the future direction to be taken also represent an internal tension within the group that initiated and organized the conferences. The deaths of Eric Miller and Rafael Moses marked the end of an era in the history of the conferences. The group then turned to Anton Obholzer, former Director of the Tavistock Clinic, and a man with a great deal of Group Relations experience, to take over as director of the conference. Beyond his proven expertise, the appointment of Anton Obholzer represented two further dimensions: First, the continued need for the presence of an Other (or as Eric Miller referred to it, a "neither") who is neither German nor Israeli/Jewish. Secondly, it signaled the potential movement in the direction of expanding the conference aim and definition beyond what it had been up to that point.

The time that has elapsed since then, though not part of the materials this book is based on, makes it possible to review briefly the developments that have taken place. The very first decision taken was to continue with the general task and aim of the conferences, with a few minor experimental changes. These changes found expression in the title of the conference, which hitherto was *"Germans and Israelis: The Past in the Present"*. The title of the fourth and fifth conferences was changed in three significant respects: It openly addressed Jews, rather than Israelis, so as to include Diaspora Jews. It also openly addressed "Others" who feel related or affected by the events of the Holocaust. Finally, it incorporated the future dimension, expanding the hitherto past-present definition. The revised title thus read: *"Shaping the Future by Confronting the Past: Germans, Jews, and Affected Others."* A further important change was the venue: It was held in Cyprus, a place that though not entirely "neutral", was neither German nor Israeli, and has had a bitter history of enmity and warring between national groups. Two conferences took place already under the new banner, venue and leadership – in 2004 and 2006. They were well attended, vigorous and exciting.

Following the 2006 Cyprus conference, the staff group that had been responsible for keeping the initiative alive and organizing each conference, decided to institutionalize itself formally as a non-profit organization with the name: *"Partners in Confronting Collective Atrocities"*, or PCCA for short. The organization is registered in Germany and maintains its website at: http://www.p-cca.org/.

The name adopted by the new organization reflects the need to go beyond the confines of the German-Jewish/Israeli issue and deal with "the rest of the world" as well. This shift rests upon the realization, already mentioned, that the conference methodology is to be regarded as highly relevant and applicable to other situations and circumstances in which different national, ethnic or religious groups are committing violence and atrocities to each other. There are obviously numerous such instances in the present day world, and the PCCA believes that the kind of work described in these pages could be of great value and benefit to them. An immediate example was the next (September 2008) conference sponsored by PCCA as a continuation and development of the two previous Cyprus conferences. The title this time was: *"Repeating, Reflecting, Moving On: Germans, Jews, Israelis, Palestinians and Others Today."*

At the same time, the PCCA is very mindful and committed to the centrality and uniqueness of the Holocaust and its aftermath. While expanding its horizons and focus, it remains convinced that the Holocaust and what it stands for have enormously and irreparably affected the present world, and that its radioactive fallout reaches areas far removed from the original site of the devastation. The adherence to this view continues to inform our understanding not only of what was done already, but what still sorely needs to be done.

This book is dedicated to this conviction.

References

Beland, H. et al. (1984): Psychoanalyse unter Hitler – Psychoanalyse Heute. Podiumsdiskussion. PSYCHE 40, 1986, 423–427.
Beland, H. (2001): Gestillt mit Tränen – Vergiftet mit Milch. Bericht von den Nazareth-Gruppenkonferenzen "Germans and Israelis – The Past in the Present". In: Bohleber, W. & Drews, S. (Eds.): Die Gegenwart der Psychoanalyse – die Psychoanalyse der Gegenwart. Stuttgart (Klett-Cotta), pp. 120–127.
Bion, W. R. (1948–51): Experiences in groups, I–VII. Human Relations, 1–4.
Bion, W. R. (1961): Experiences in Groups and Other Papers. London (Tavistock Publications).
Bion, W. R. (1952) Group dynamics: a re-view. Int. J Psycho-Anal., 33, 235–47.
Bohleber, W. & Drews, S. (Eds.) (2001): Die Gegenwart der Psychoanalyse – die Psychoanalyse der Gegenwart. Stuttgart (Klett-Cotta).
Brainin, E. & Kaminer, I. J. (1982): Psychoanalysis and Nationalsocialism. PSYCHE 36, 989–1012.
Dahmer, H. (1983): Capitulation before the Weltanschauung. Zu einem Beitrag von Carl Müller-Braunschweig aus dem Herbst 1933. PSYCHE 37, 1116–1135.
Erlich, H. S. (1997): On Discourse with an Enemy. In: Shapiro, E. R. (Ed.): The Inner World in the Outer World: Psychoanalytic Perspectives. New Haven (Yale University Press), pp. 123–142.
Erlich, H. S. (1999): The plight of Jews in Germany. An open letter. PSYCHE 53, 1188–1191.
Erlich, H. S. (2001a): Enemies Within and Without: Paranoia and Regression in Groups and Organisations. In: Gould, L. J.; Stapley L. F. & Stein, M. (Eds.): The Systems Psychodynamics of Organisations. London (Karnac), pp. 115–131.
Erlich, H. S. (2001b): Milch, Gift, Tränen. Bericht von den Nazareth-Gruppenkonferenzen "Germans and Israelis – The Past in the Present". In: Bohleber, W. & Drews, S. (Eds.): Die Gegenwart der Psychoanalyse – die Psychoanalyse der Gegenwart. Stuttgart (Klett-Cotta), pp. 128–138.
Freud, S. (1935a): Postscript to An Autobiographical Study. Standard Ed. Vol. 20, p. 71.
Klein, H. (1986): From Guilt to Responsibility. In: Luft, H. & Maas, G. (Ed.): Psychoanalytische Psychosomatik und aktuelle Probleme der Psychoanalyse. Hofheim (DER Congress), pp. 245–252.
Klein, H. & Erlich, H. S. (1976): Some psychoanalytic structural aspects of family function and growth. Adolescent Psychiat. 6, 171–194.

Klein, M. (1959): Our adult world and its roots in infancy. Human Relations 12, 291–303. Also in Klein, M. (1963): Our Adult World and Other Essays, London (Heinemann), pp. 1–22.

Lohmann, H. M. & Rosenkötter, L. (1982): Psychoanalysis in Hitler's Germany. Wie war es wirklich? PSYCHE 36, 961–988.

Miller, E. J. (1989): The 'Leicester' Model: Experiential Study of Group and Organizational Processes. Occasional Paper no. 10. Tavistock, Institute of Human Relations.

Miller, E. J. & Rice, A. K. (1967): Systems of Organization: Task and Sentient Systems and their Boundary Control. London (Tavistock Publications).

Moses, R. & Moses-Hrushovski, R. (1986): A form of denial at the Hamburg Congress. Intern. Rev. Psychoanal. 13, 175–180.

Rice, A. K. (1958): Productivity and Social Organization: The Ahmedabad Experiment. London (Tavistock Publications). Reprinted: New York and London (Garland Publishing), 1987.

Rice, A. K. (1963): The Enterprise and its Environment. London (Tavistock Publications).

Rice, A. K. (1965): Learning for Leadership. London (Tavistock Publications).

Rossier, N. (1986): Bamberg – Erinnerungen an eine Arbeitstagung. In: Henseler, H. & Kuchenbuch, A. (Eds.): Die Wiederkehr von Krieg und Verfolgung in Psychoanalysen. Ulm (DPV), pp. 84–86.

Rüsen, J. (2001): Holocaust-Erfahrung und deutsche Identität. Ideen zu einer Typologie der Generationen. In: Bohleber, W. & Drews, S. (Eds.): Die Gegenwart der Psychoanalyse – die Psychoanalyse der Gegenwart. Stuttgart (Klett-Cotta).

Vogt, R. (1986): Psychoanalyse unter Hitler – Psychoanalyse heute. In: Beland, H. et al. (1986): Podiumsdiskussion. PSYCHE 40, 435–436.

2002 · 378 Seiten · Broschur
ISBN 978-3-89806-282-4

2004 · 198 Seiten · gebunden
ISBN 978-3-89806-372-2

Terrorism, Jihad, and Sacred Vengeance delves into the psychology of terrorism and religious violence. What comprise the ideas, impulses and fantasies of terrorists and suicide bombers? How do victimization and exposure to death affect the psyche? From fascistic and paranoid responses following September 11th, 2001, to dreams of entering Paradise and blissfully joining God through acts of self-destruction, to the symbolism of evil and sacrifice, Terrorism, Jihad, and Sacred Vengeance explores the madness and despair persisting in the wake of recent events.

Critics have called the book Narcissism and Power (2002), written by Hans-Jürgen Wirth, a »masterpiece of political psychology«. In 9/11 as a Collective Trauma he presents a collection of his most interesting essays about psyche and politics. He reflects on the psychic structure of suicide bombers and analyzes the psycho-political causes and the consequences of the Iraq War. The other essays focus on xenophobia and violence, the story of Jewish psychoanalysts who emigrated to the United States from Nazi Germany, and the idea of man in psychoanalysis.

P🕮V
Psychosozial-Verlag

Goethestr. 29 · 35390 Gießen · Tel. 0641/9716903 · Fax 77742
bestellung@psychosozial-verlag.de
www.psychosozial-verlag.de

2006 · 216 Seiten · Broschur
ISBN 978-3-89806-438-5

2007 · 186 Seiten · Broschur
ISBN 978-3-89806-508-5

The Psychology of Personal Constructs, as devised by the American psychologist George Kelly, stresses the importance of the meanings that individuals attach to persons and events in the world surrounding them. Originating in clinical psychology, it has increasingly attracted the interest of scholars and practitioners working in education, in organisations, and in other disciplines working with people. As there are hardly more »personal« processes than creative ones, it seems appropriate to look at the arts from a personal construct psychology perspective. This book presents for the first time analyses of creative processes, but it features also personal accounts by creative people – who write, sing, dance, act, and make music.

Migration and persecution are of central importance in our culture not only in Europe, but across the globe. In this book, six psychoanalysts seek a personal theoretical and clinical approach to the subject and provide an access to the heterogeneous forms and treatment of the human experience with uprooting, trauma, loss and violence. The variety of this book offers a lifelike approach both to the topic of migration and persecution and to how the fear of the foreign and the strange is dealt with.

P🕮V
Psychosozial-Verlag

Goethestr. 29 · 35390 Gießen · Tel. 0641/9716903 · Fax 77742
bestellung@psychosozial-verlag.de
www.psychosozial-verlag.de

www.ingramcontent.com/pod-product-compliance
Ingram Content Group UK Ltd.
Pitfield, Milton Keynes, MK11 3LW, UK
UKHW041947230426
12048UKWH00008B/188